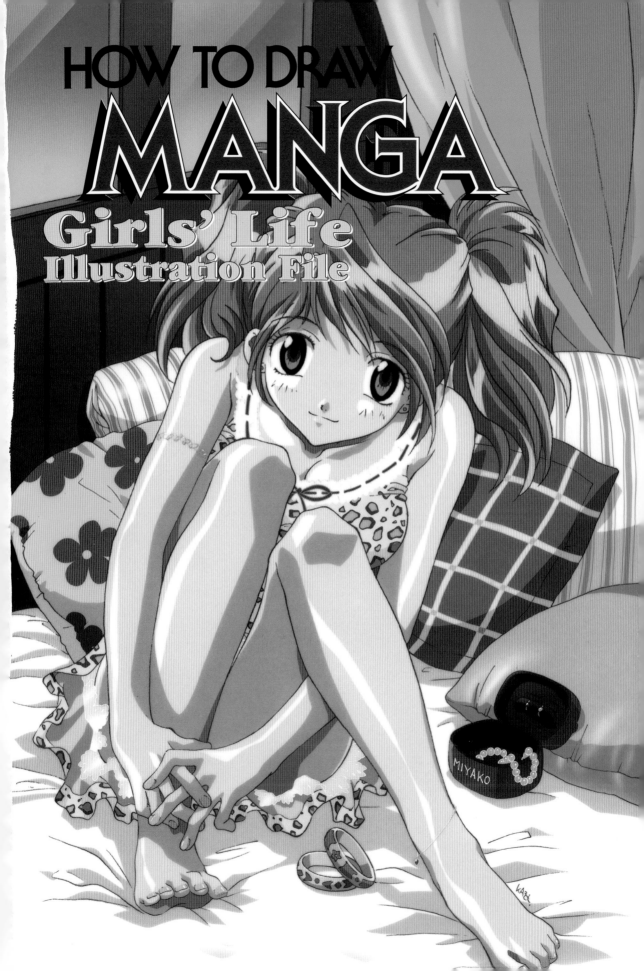

HOW TO DRAW MANGA: Girls' Life Illustration File
by Kazuko Tadano

Copyright © 2000 Kazuko Tadano
Copyright © 2000 Graphic-sha Publishing Co., Ltd.

This book was first designed and produced by Graphic-sha Publishing Co., Ltd.
in Japan in 2000. This English edition was published by Graphic-sha Publishing Co., Ltd.
in Japan in 2003.

Graphic-sha Publishing Co., Ltd.
1-14-17 Kudan-kita, Chiyoda-ku, Tokyo 102-0073 Japan

Cell artist: Rumiko Nagai
CG colorist: Minme Nanigashi
Back ground artist: Manami Koyama
Assistants: BEN², Sayuri Takahashi, Hiromi Handa, Hiromi Matsushita
Main title logo design: Hideyuki Amemura
Planning editor: Sahoko Hyakutake (Graphic-sha Publishing Co., Ltd.)
English edition Editor: Glenn Kardy (Japanime Co., Ltd.)
English edition layout: Yuuki Saito (Palette)
English translaion management: Língua fránca, Inc. (an3y-skmt@asahi-net.or.jp)
Foreign language edition project coordinator: Kumiko Sakamoto (Graphic-sha Publishing Co., Ltd.)

Distributed by
Japanime Co., Ltd.
2-8-102 Naka-cho, Kawaguchi-shi,
Saitama 332-0022, Japan
Phone /Fax: +81-(0)48-259-3444
E-mail: sales@japanime.com
http:// www.Japanime.com

First printing: May 2003

ISBN: 4-7661-1338-1
Printed and bound in China by Everbest Printing Co., Ltd.

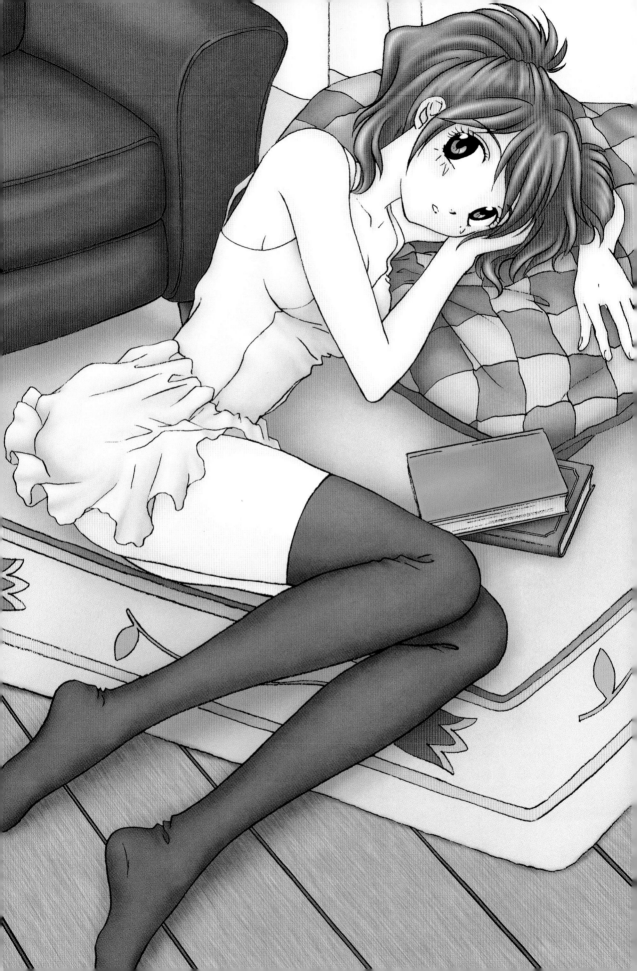

Foreword

The publisher and I first began discussing the concept of this book in the summer of 1999. Our goal was to provide a glimpse into the lifestyles of various types of female characters. Coincidentally, at the same time I began working on the book, I was also in the process of introducing several characters on my website. These new characters seemed perfect for this type of book, and so they ended up being the models I used. While no mention of it is made in this volume, each and every one has a name. The perky girl is Miyako Himekawa. The sporty one is Mai Oribe. The dreamy lass is Sayo Koishikawa. The precocious gal is Ayame Hojo, while the shy one is her twin sister and polar opposite, Suzuna. Last but not least is the uppity girl, Kyoka Saianji.

This is the first time I have ever published a book of this sort, so I am feeling just a bit apprehensive. I sincerely hope my readers will find it useful.

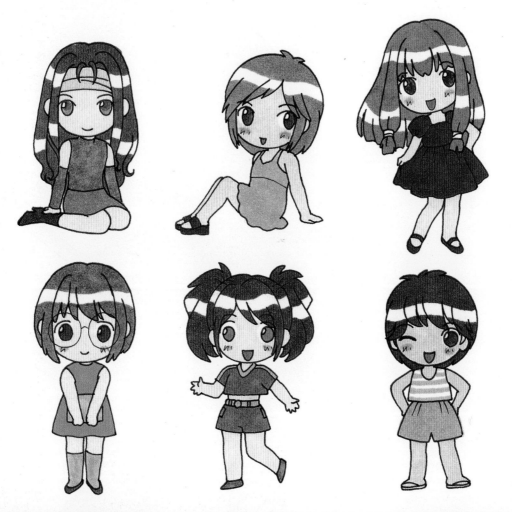

Table of Contents

Cast of Characters

The apartments and items appearing in this book are all based on those of young women whom I actually know. Six general character types are featured in this book. When creating your own character, think about the young women close to you, and select the type of character in this book that appeals to you the most.

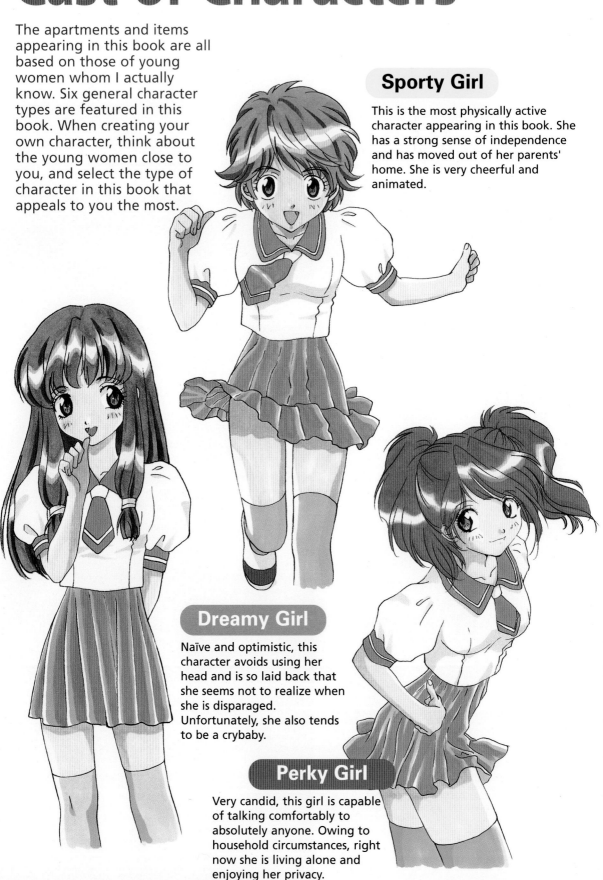

Sporty Girl

This is the most physically active character appearing in this book. She has a strong sense of independence and has moved out of her parents' home. She is very cheerful and animated.

Dreamy Girl

Naïve and optimistic, this character avoids using her head and is so laid back that she seems not to realize when she is disparaged. Unfortunately, she also tends to be a crybaby.

Perky Girl

Very candid, this girl is capable of talking comfortably to absolutely anyone. Owing to household circumstances, right now she is living alone and enjoying her privacy.

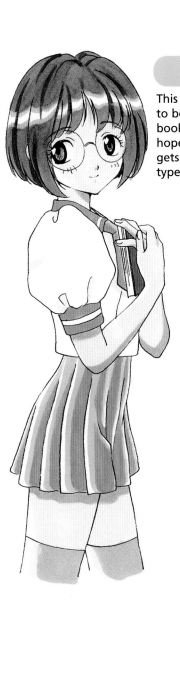

Shy Girl

This girl is rather timid and tends to be clumsy with words. A fan of books (especially horror), she hopes to become a writer. She gets along well with outgoing types.

Precocious Girl

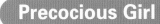

Given to making risqué comments without batting an eye, this girl puts those around her on edge. She would never admit it herself, but she can be something of a geek.

Uppity Girl

This character has the pride true to a girl of privileged upbringing —and a temper to boot. But she often feels lonely and is somewhat spoiled. She certainly feels the need for attention, so from time to time behaves like a little brat.

Basic Character Design I

Learning to Draw the Characters

Step-by-Step

① First, make a rough sketch of the character, getting a general idea of the pose you want.

② Adjust the proportions and add details to the drawing.

③ Prepare a clean line drawing using a mechanical pencil, and make a photocopy.

④ Use markers to color the photocopied drawing, and yor're done!

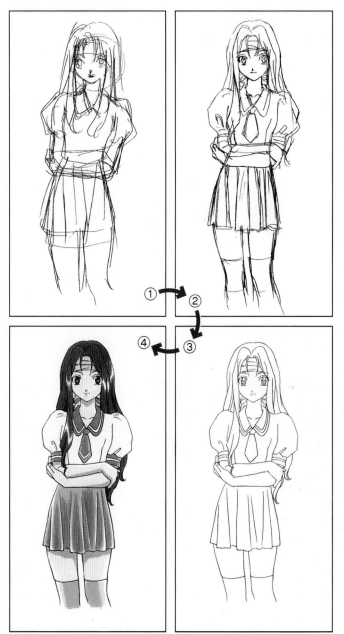

Character Design and Sketches

In general, an artist will visualize in his or her mind how a character will be posed and then put it to paper. However, doing so isn't always easy. That is where photography journals and magazine ads come in handy. They can give you a better idea of how to make a character's pose look natural. Once you've pretty much decided how you want to pose your character, study the human models in those photographs. Remember, though, that some angles work well in photography but not in drawing. Don't fall into the trap of simply copying the poses you see in photographs—you will need to trust your artistic sense, too!

Rough sketches and Line Drawings

You may find this hard to believe, but I do the majority of my work—including rough sketches and line drawings—with mechanical pencils. They are lightweight, and I particularly like the kind that have a rubberized finger grip. Since very little pressure needs to be applied when drawing with such pencils, a soft #3B lead works well. (I have experimented with various leads and found those manufactured by Uni tend to be the best in terms of softness.) I do occasionally use pens, but I prefer the soft touch of a pencil and tend to reach for that first.

Colors

I use Copic and Triart markers, layering and gradating the colors. (All of the color work in this book was done with markers.) I also frequently use colored screen tones manufactured by Deleter and Maxon. Deleter tones work well because the adhesive backing is not as sticky as that on other brand tones, thus allowing for easy removal from the drawing should I make a mistake. However, Deleter does not offer as much color options, so I also use the stickier Maxon tones. The adhesive used by Maxon is so strong that it is impossible to remove the tones without damaging the illustration, so be sure you get it right the first time!

Materials and Tools
- Mechanical pencil (#3B lead)
- Color Markers (Copic and Triart)
- Color tone (Deleter and Maxon)
- Photocopier (Worth purchasing your own)

Home Sweet Home

Chapter 1

Layout and Illustrations

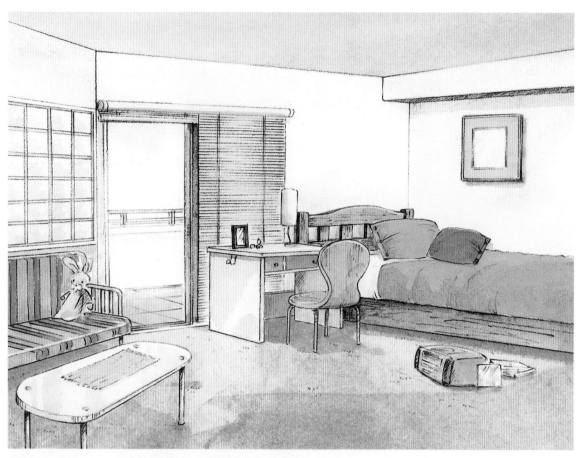

Perky Girl's Room

This charming apartment is rather unusual, as not too many teen-age girls live alone. The furnishings are functional yet brightly colored, reflecting the pleasant personality of the occupant.

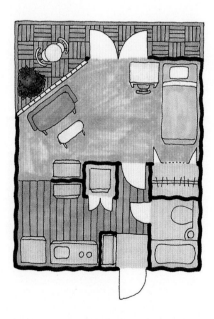

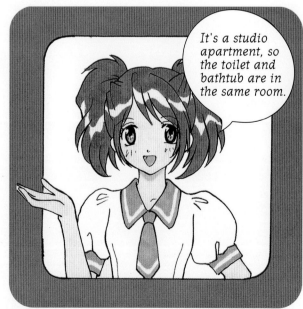

It's a studio apartment, so the toilet and bathtub are in the same room.

Note: In a typical Japanese home, the toilet and bathtub are normally located in small, separate rooms.

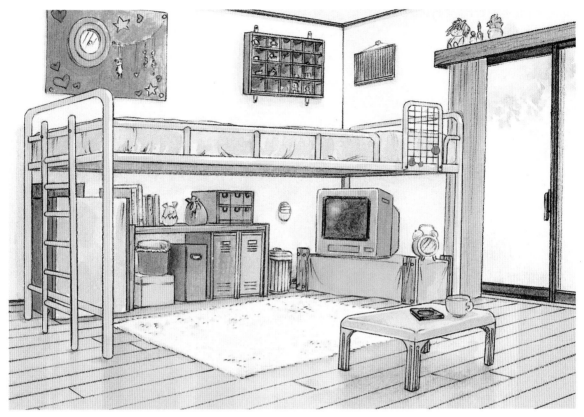

Sporty Girl's Room

The interior has pop-culture influences. A good portion of the furnishings required self-assembly, which was no problem for this girl! She has a passion for knickknacks and is now plagued by overflowing shelves.

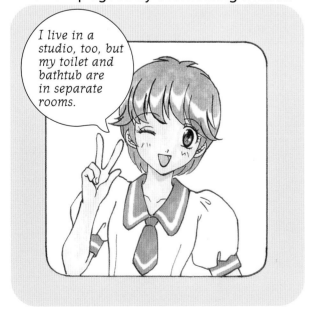

I live in a studio, too, but my toilet and bathtub are in separate rooms.

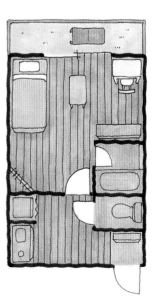

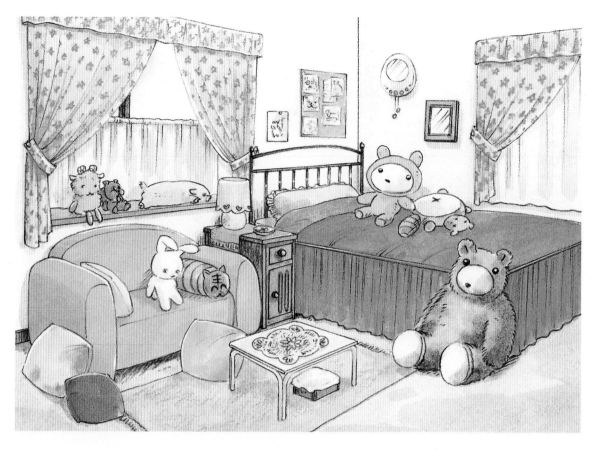

Dreamy Girl's Room

This bedroom has fairy-tale overtones and is cluttered with girly objects. Plush animals are indispensable to the scene. The resident's favorite is the oversized teddy bear.

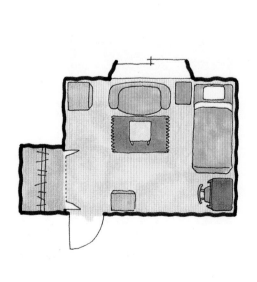

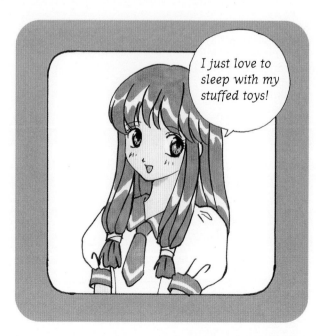

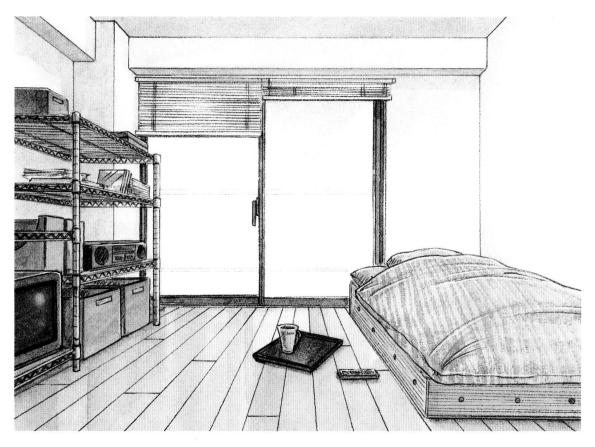

Precocious Girl's Room

The interior reflects a skillful and optimal use of space. Monotone colors give the room a somewhat masculine feel, but unlike a boy's room, this one is tidy.

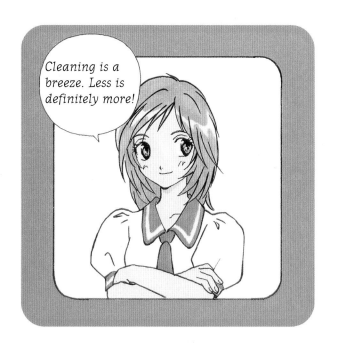

Cleaning is a breeze. Less is definitely more!

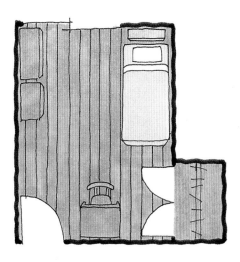

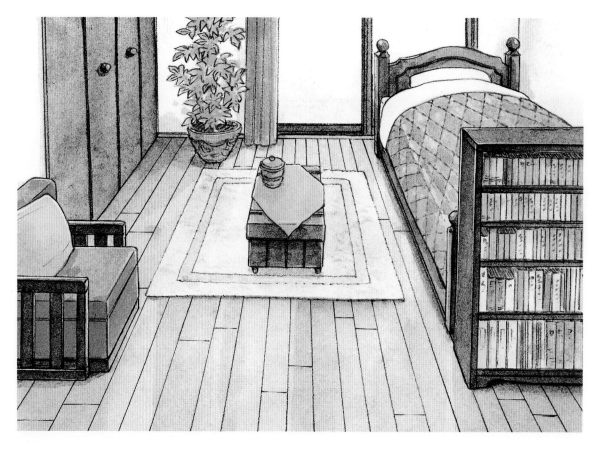

Shy Girl's Room

The furnishings are woody, and mostly have a down-to-earth feel. Potted plants are integral. She is an avid reader, so the large bookshelf is a must.

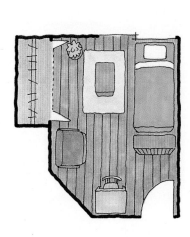

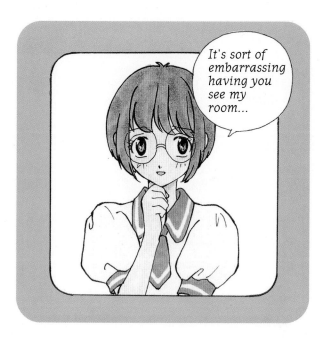

It's sort of embarrassing having you see my room...

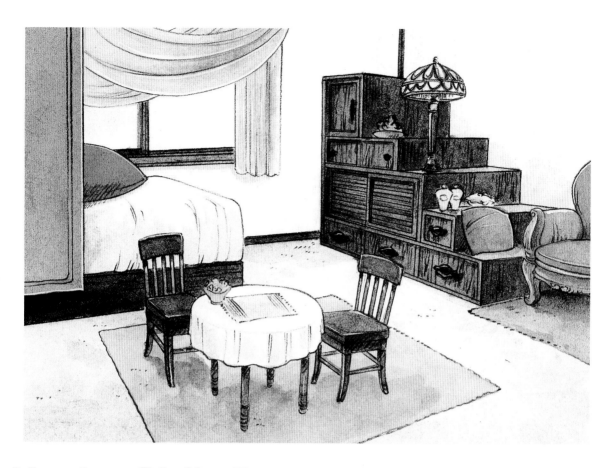

Uppity Girl's Room

This room is rather large by Japanese standards. The furnishings are kept to a minimum to avoid clutter. The large closet by the door completes the scene.

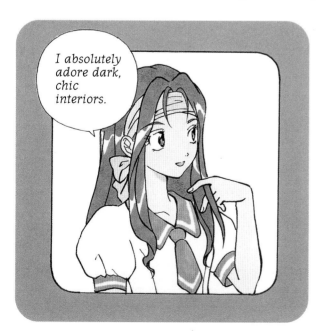

I absolutely adore dark, chic interiors.

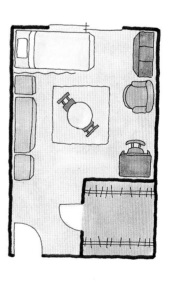

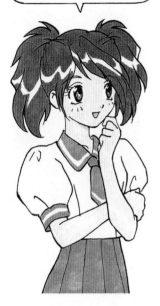

I have enough basic appliances to make simple dishes, but what I really want now is an oven.

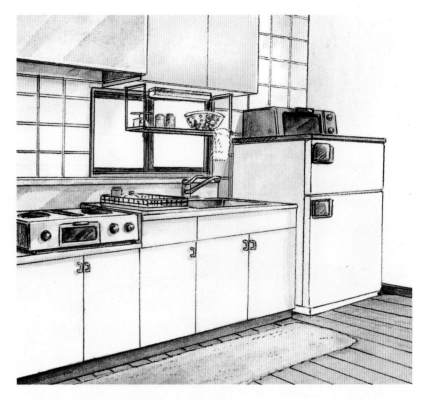

A Look at the Single Girl's Kitchen

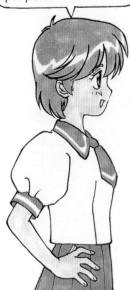

This is a pretty cramped, minimalistic kitchen. But I really don't cook all that much, so it serves its purpose.

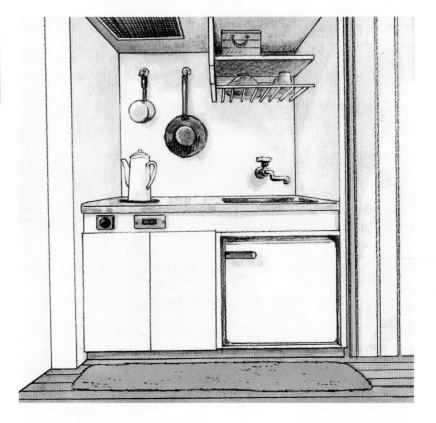

❏ *The Foyer*

Perky Girl

I live in a studio apartment, so the foyer is tiny. I decorated the top of the shoe closet with some cut sunflowers and colored beads for a seasonal effect. I also coordinated a light switch cover with a mirror in an alternating-tile pattern.

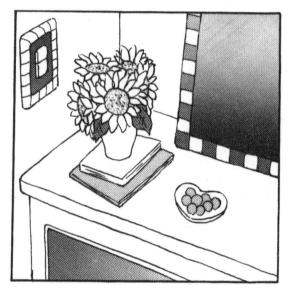

Shoes:
I approach my shoes playfully and select the ones I'm going to wear based on a color or style that matches my mood. I wear everything from flats to dressy heels.

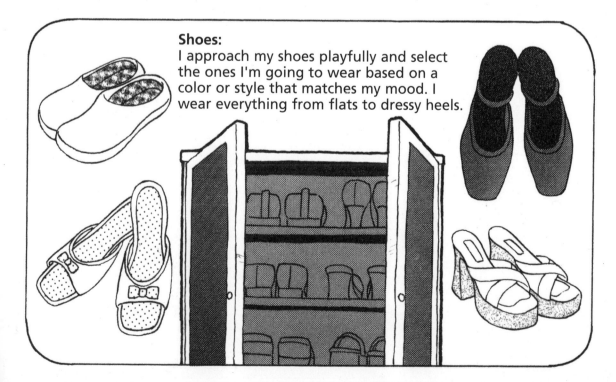

Sporty Girl

My apartment is intended for one person, so the foyer is rather cramped. Consequently, my shoe closet is smaller than usual. I decorated the top with watches, nametags and pins to give it a cheerful touch.

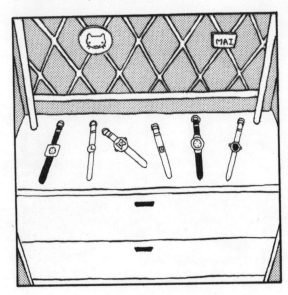

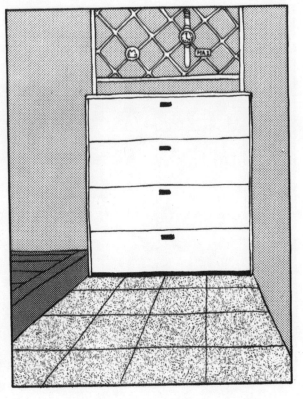

Shoes
I prefer casual shoes. Sneakers that you can just slip on are where it's at as far as I'm concerned.

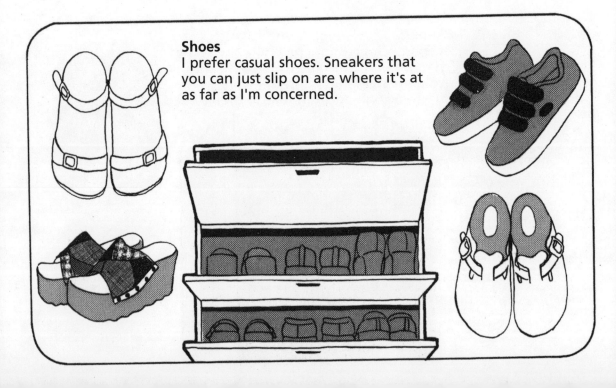

Dreamy Girl

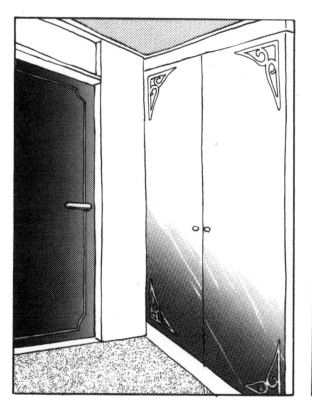

I still live with my parents, and the foyer in our home is rather large. Our shoe closet is built into the wall, and the door has mirrors. We added fancy stickers to the doors to make the entrance a little more elegant.

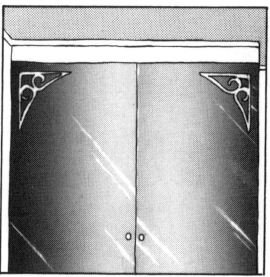

Shoes:
I have a penchant for cute boots and tend to buy on impulse. But sometimes I find out later on that they don't fit all that well, so some never really leave the box.

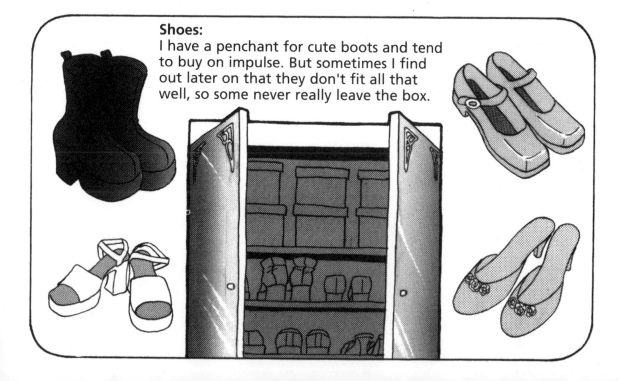

Precocious Girl

This is a family condominium, so our foyer is nice and roomy. We have space for our shoes in another closet, so I only keep the ones I wear the most in the foyer.

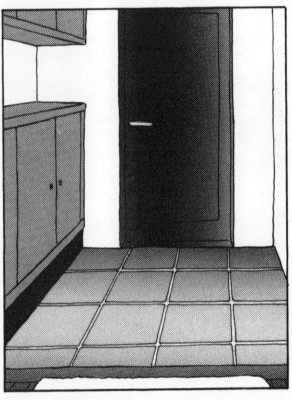

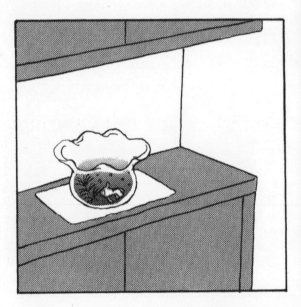

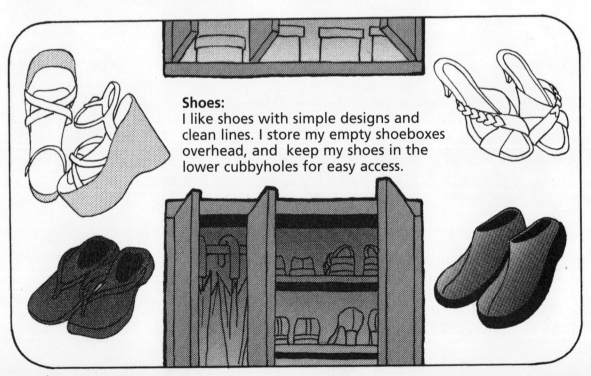

Shoes:
I like shoes with simple designs and clean lines. I store my empty shoeboxes overhead, and keep my shoes in the lower cubbyholes for easy access.

Shy Girl

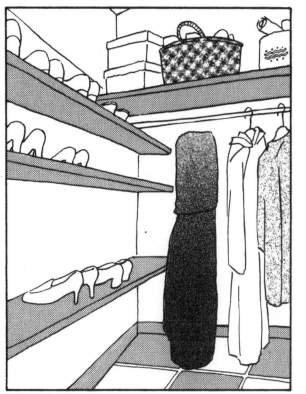

I keep my dress shoes, coats and gardening tools in this closet. It is walk-in style, which makes it really convenient.

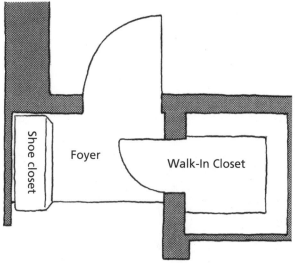

Shoe closet

Foyer

Walk-In Closet

Items Stored in the Walk-In Closet

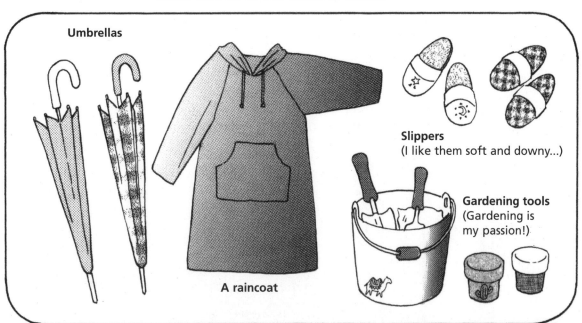

Umbrellas

A raincoat

Slippers
(I like them soft and downy...)

Gardening tools
(Gardening is
my passion!)

Uppity Girl

I live in a huge house, so the foyer is naturally spacious. This chest serves as our shoe closet. We keep potpourris—homemade, of course—on the top.

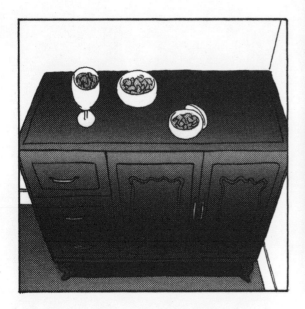

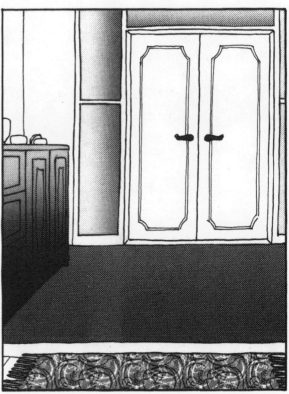

Shoes:
Most of my shoes are dressy; I rarely wear athletic shoes. I keep cases of lotions and other cosmetics and a few fold-up umbrellas in my drawer so I can grab them on the go.

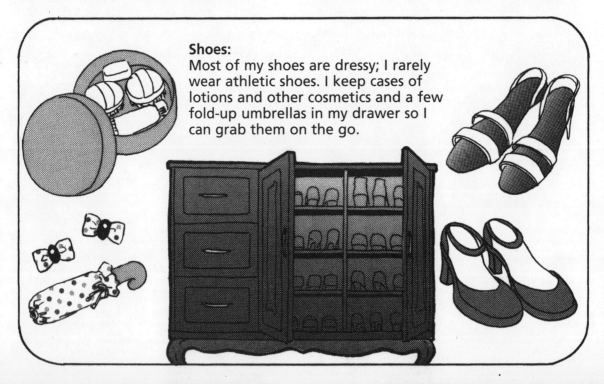

❏ A Peek into the Closet

Perky Girl

I have a built-in closet. It's a bit on the small side, but since I don't own a lot of clothes, it suits me just fine.

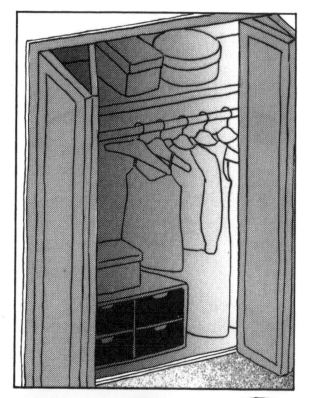

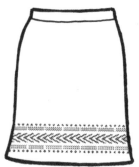

Most of my clothes are dresses, but I like casual stuff too.

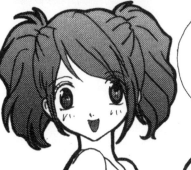

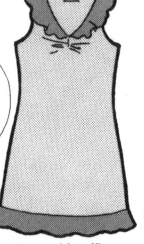
Bordered skirt

Denim skirt

Dress with ruffles

Polka-dot dress

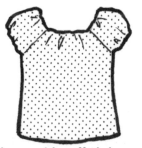
Blouse with puffed sleeves

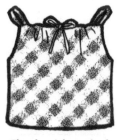
Checkered camisole

Sporty Girl

I don't have a closet, as it would just make my apartment more cramped than it already is. Instead, I wedged a pole into a corner and hang my clothes from it. I keep other clothes in a wicker basket. I sure know how to save space!

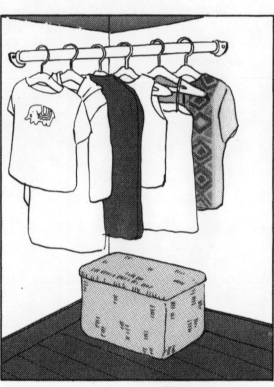

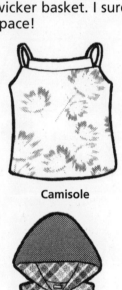

Camisole

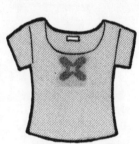

Baby doll T-shirt

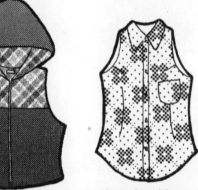

Sleeveless hooded jacket

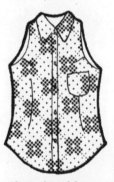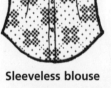

Sleeveless blouse

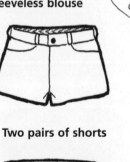

Two pairs of shorts

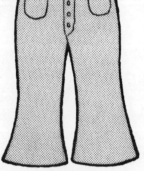

Bell-bottoms

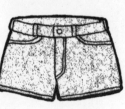

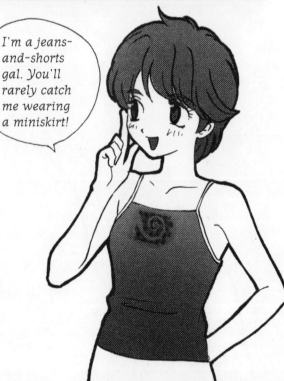

I'm a jeans-and-shorts gal. You'll rarely catch me wearing a miniskirt!

Dreamy Girl

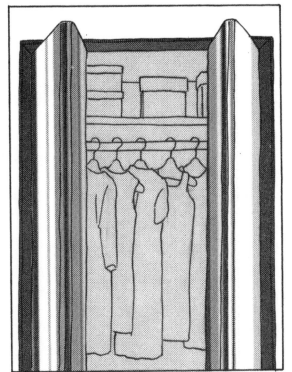

My closet is average-sized, but I stuff it with way too many clothes. I just can't seem to fit everything in! Maybe if I had another closet...

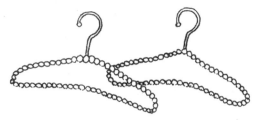

Beaded hangers (I really love these.)

I like to wear miniskirts or really cute dresses, but every now and then I wear pants.

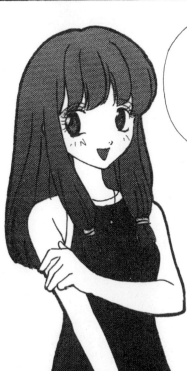

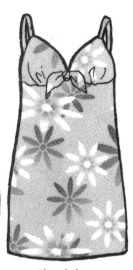

Floral dress

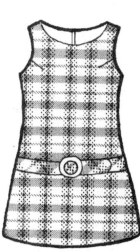

Drop-waist dress

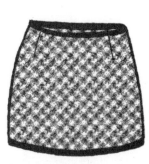

Miniskirt

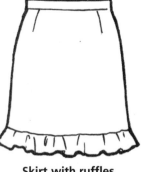

Skirt with ruffles

Precocious Girl

I have a built-in closet. It isn't exactly roomy, but since I make a point of only keeping the essentials, it's more than enough for me.

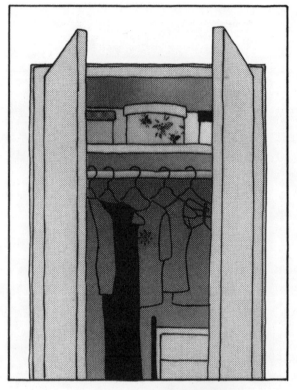

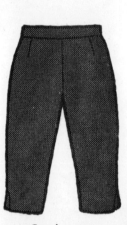

Capri pants

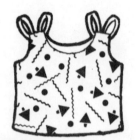

Camisole-and-skirt ensemble

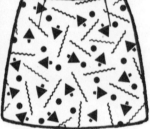

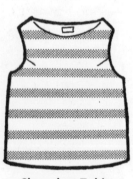

Sleeveless T-shirt

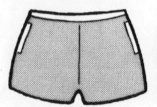

Shorts

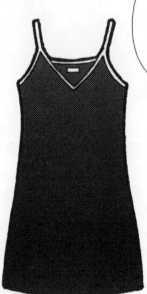

Spaghetti-strap dress

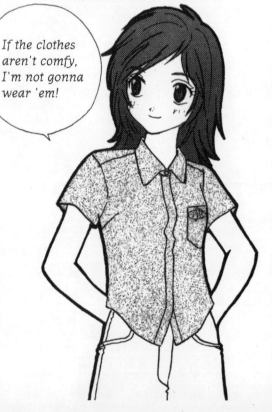

If the clothes aren't comfy, I'm not gonna wear 'em!

Shy Girl

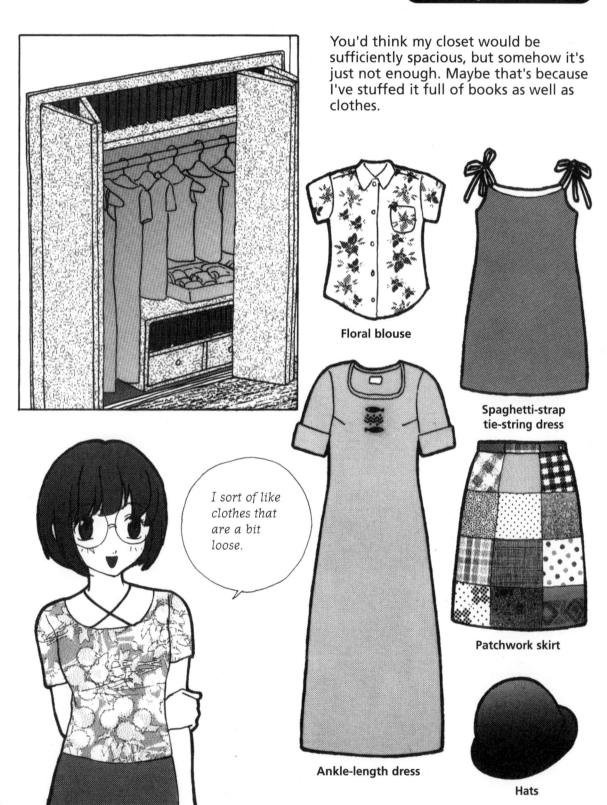

You'd think my closet would be sufficiently spacious, but somehow it's just not enough. Maybe that's because I've stuffed it full of books as well as clothes.

Floral blouse

Spaghetti-strap tie-string dress

I sort of like clothes that are a bit loose.

Patchwork skirt

Ankle-length dress

Hats

Uppity Girl

I have a huge walk-in closet, so storage is not a problem. I could probably fit in enough clothes to last me five seasons a year!

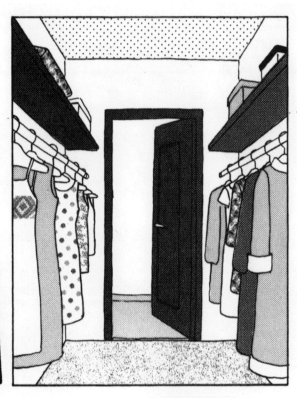

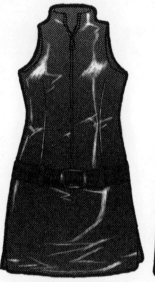

Leather dress

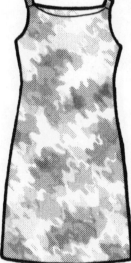

Semi-formal dress

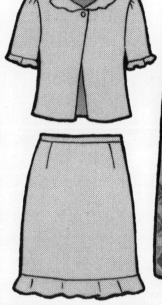

Blouse-and-skirt ensemble

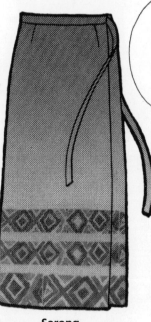

Sarong

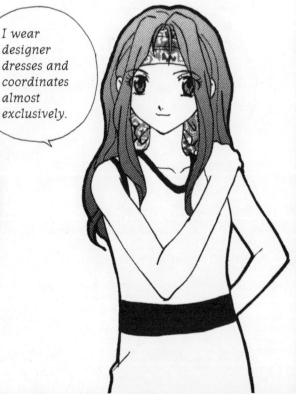

I wear designer dresses and coordinates almost exclusively.

❑ *Around the Dressing Table*

I don't have a dressing table, since extra furniture would make my already small studio even more cramped. I keep my cosmetics on the sink next to my bathtub. My favorite brand of makeup? None, really.

Perky Girl

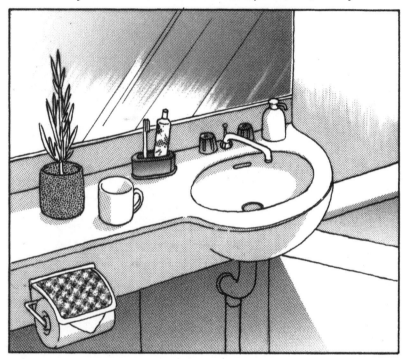

I don't wear much anyway. My skin does tend to be on the dry side, though, so I often use a moisturizer.

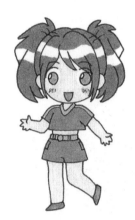

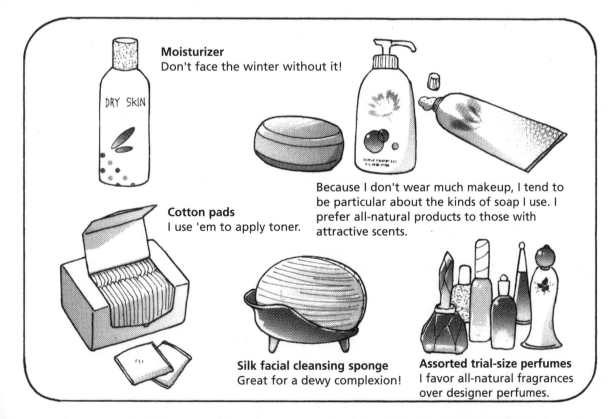

Moisturizer
Don't face the winter without it!

Cotton pads
I use 'em to apply toner.

Because I don't wear much makeup, I tend to be particular about the kinds of soap I use. I prefer all-natural products to those with attractive scents.

DRY SKIN

Silk facial cleansing sponge
Great for a dewy complexion!

Assorted trial-size perfumes
I favor all-natural fragrances over designer perfumes.

Sporty Girl

I converted this old bookshelf into a dressing table simply by sticking a small mirror on top. I keep my cosmetics and other personal item in a wicker basket.

My apartment is a little cramped for space, so I have to make do. Still, all I ever really do is wash my face and head out the door. I'll wait until I'm older and really need cosmetics before I begin using them regularly.

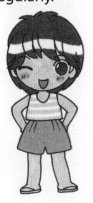

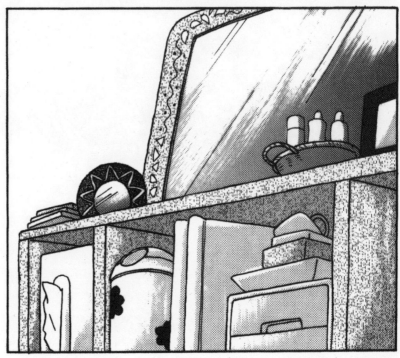

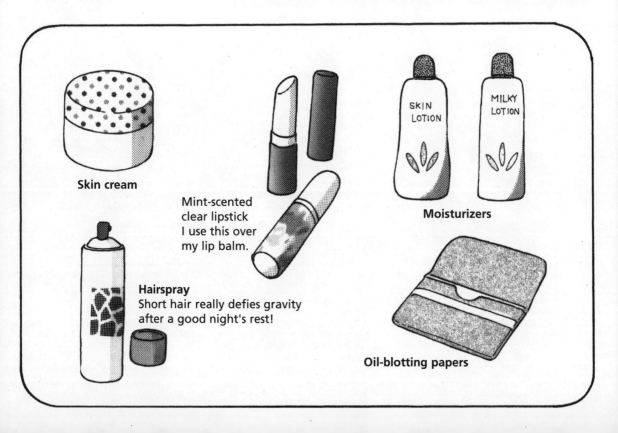

Skin cream

Mint-scented clear lipstick
I use this over my lip balm.

Moisturizers

Hairspray
Short hair really defies gravity after a good night's rest!

Oil-blotting papers

I created my dressing table by placing a medium-sized mirror on top of a sideboard with glass doors. This is perfectly fine for looking at my face.

Dreamy Girl

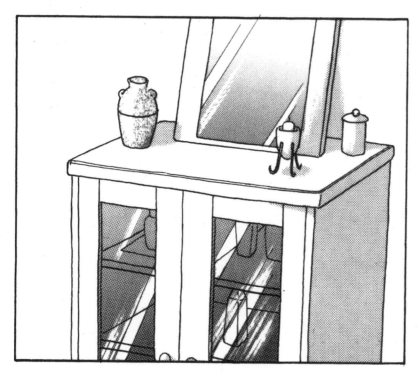

If I want to see my entire reflection, there is always the full-length mirror in the foyer. Right now, I'm obsessed with nail art and have lots of false nails. I plan on entering a contest once I come up with a really interesting design of my own.

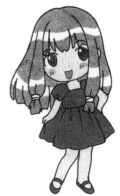

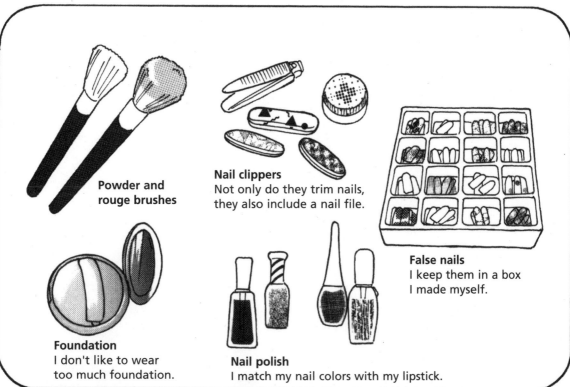

Powder and rouge brushes

Nail clippers
Not only do they trim nails, they also include a nail file.

False nails
I keep them in a box I made myself.

Foundation
I don't like to wear too much foundation.

Nail polish
I match my nail colors with my lipstick.

Precocious Girl

I have a full-length mirror simply propped up against a wall. I can get dressed and do my makeup with just this one mirror. I believe that beauty starts from the inside, so I don't own many cosmetics. Instead, I use an assortment of vitamin supplements.

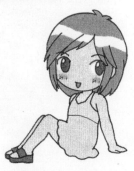

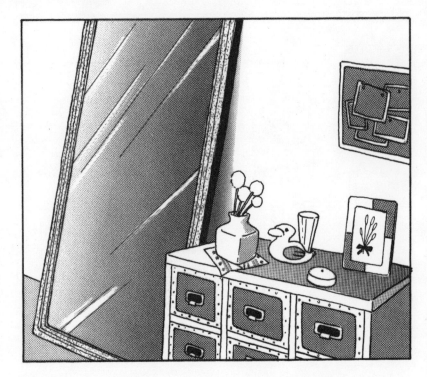

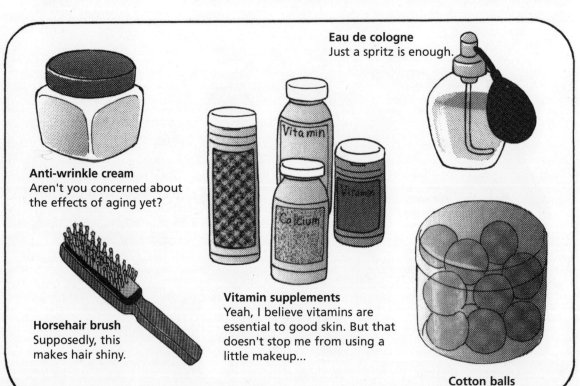

Eau de cologne
Just a spritz is enough.

Anti-wrinkle cream
Aren't you concerned about the effects of aging yet?

Horsehair brush
Supposedly, this makes hair shiny.

Vitamin supplements
Yeah, I believe vitamins are essential to good skin. But that doesn't stop me from using a little makeup...

Cotton balls

I keep my cosmetics in a medicine cabinet. I find it particularly functional, since it doesn't take up floor space. The antique design really appeals to me.

Shy Girl

I have sensitive skin, so I don't use much makeup. Instead, I use a mild baby lotion. When I'm in the mood to paint my nails, I tend toward light pink colors. I stay away from colognes and prefer instead the scent of soap.

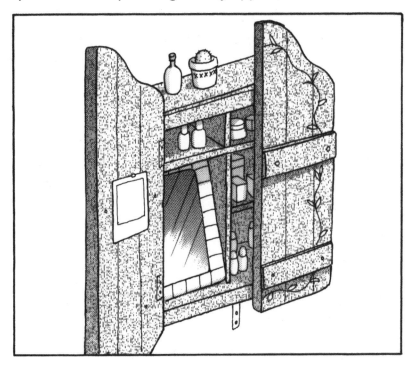

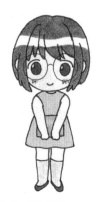

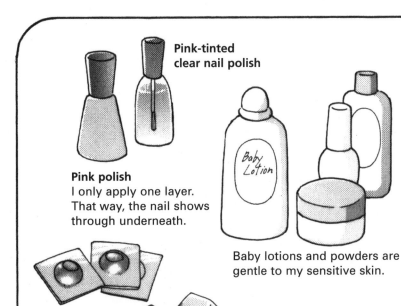

Pink-tinted clear nail polish

Pink polish
I only apply one layer. That way, the nail shows through underneath.

Baby lotions and powders are gentle to my sensitive skin.

My lips are fairly light in color, so I use a lightly tinted lipstick.

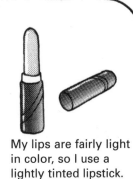

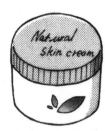

99% organic skin cream

Disposable contact lenses
Sometimes I leave my glasses at home when I go out.

Uppity Girl

I have a vanity with a tilt-up mirror designed specifically for applying cosmetics. There are nine compartments underneath, so I can categorize my makeup.

Right now, I am interested in skin-lightening cosmetics, so that is what comprises most of what I own. But are they effective? Well, sort of... I also tend to use name-brand cosmetics.

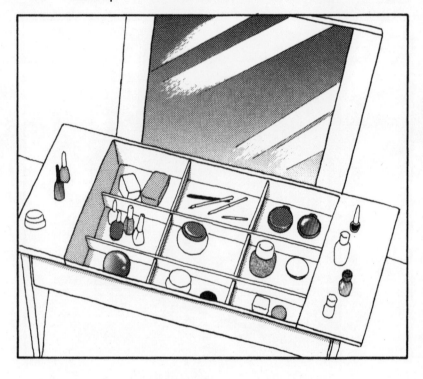

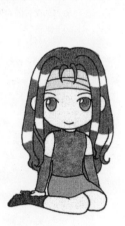

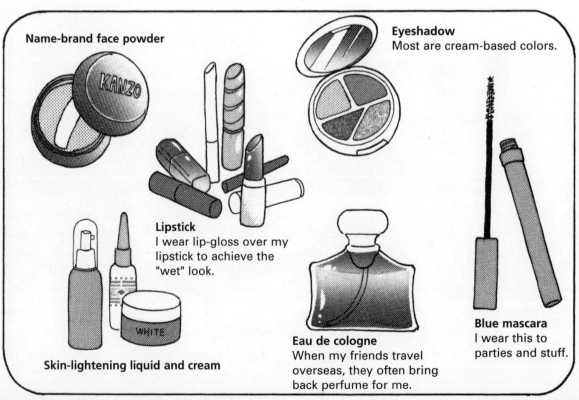

Name-brand face powder

Eyeshadow
Most are cream-based colors.

Lipstick
I wear lip-gloss over my lipstick to achieve the "wet" look.

Skin-lightening liquid and cream

Eau de cologne
When my friends travel overseas, they often bring back perfume for me.

Blue mascara
I wear this to parties and stuff.

❏ *Inside the Desk*

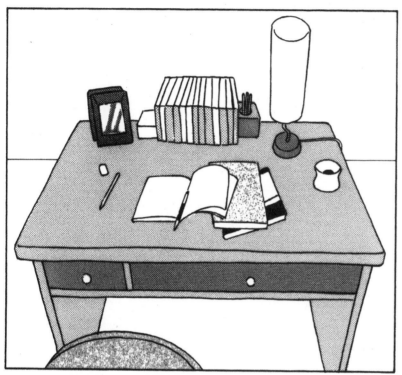

This doubles as my nightstand, so I avoid cluttering it with things. I like to make my own notebooks out of scrap paper, and I have a sticker dispenser that I just cherish. I also make personalized stickers, which I give out to my friends. I have any number of colored markers, which I use for drawing pictures.

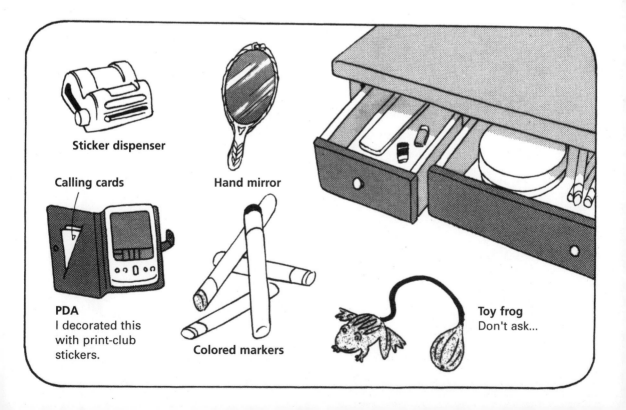

Sticker dispenser

Calling cards

Hand mirror

PDA
I decorated this with print-club stickers.

Colored markers

Toy frog
Don't ask...

Sporty Girl

I have my very own computer! I'm having a great time surfing the Net. But I really want to have my own website. Everything on my desk is somehow computer-related. I wonder if this is what an office desk is like. On the other hand, maybe it just makes me seem like an old, balding accountant...

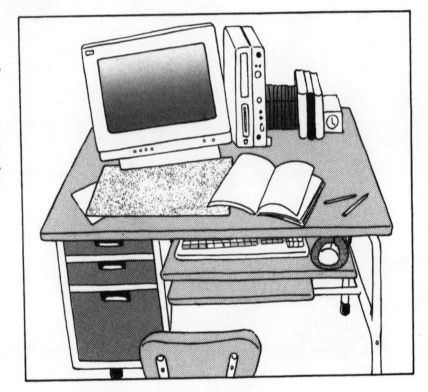

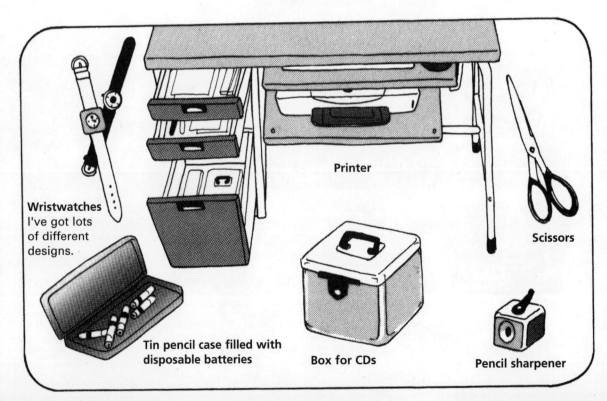

Wristwatches
I've got lots of different designs.

Printer

Scissors

Tin pencil case filled with disposable batteries

Box for CDs

Pencil sharpener

Dreamy Girl

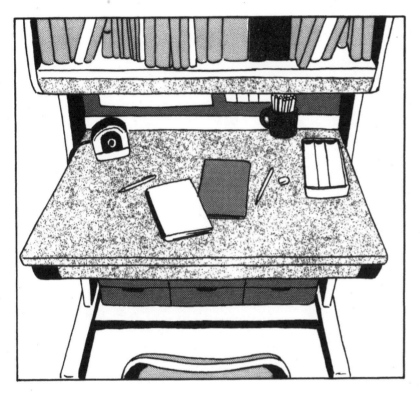

This is a pretty typical desk. It certainly seems functional. Anyway, I can put my books on the upper shelf, which is really useful for keeping them organized. I keep mostly snapshots I took myself and print-club stickers in the desk drawer. Where do I keep my homework and notebooks? Um, well... I have a pair of pinking shears to trim the borders of my print-club stickers into really cute shapes.

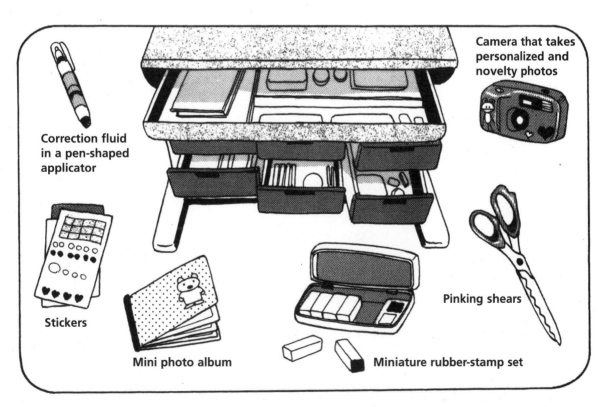

Correction fluid in a pen-shaped applicator

Camera that takes personalized and novelty photos

Stickers

Mini photo album

Miniature rubber-stamp set

Pinking shears

Precocious Girl

This is really a drafting table—the kind that professional animators use. Why did I choose this? Because it's efficient and functional. All of my friends say I'm turning into a geek, but I don't care. Unfortunately, drafting tables don't come with drawers, so I have a chest off to the side to store things. Still, it seems like all I own are office supplies. I guess I am a bit worried people are going to say I'm becoming a little old lady.

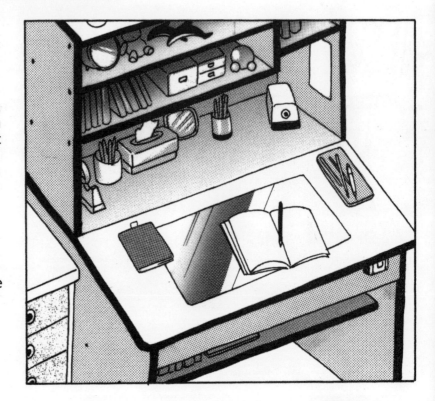

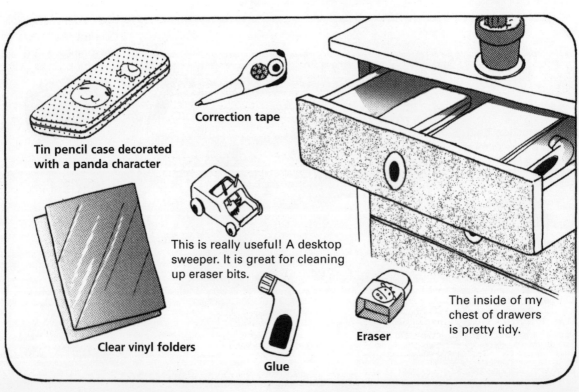

Tin pencil case decorated with a panda character

Correction tape

This is really useful! A desktop sweeper. It is great for cleaning up eraser bits.

Clear vinyl folders

Glue

Eraser

The inside of my chest of drawers is pretty tidy.

Shy Girl

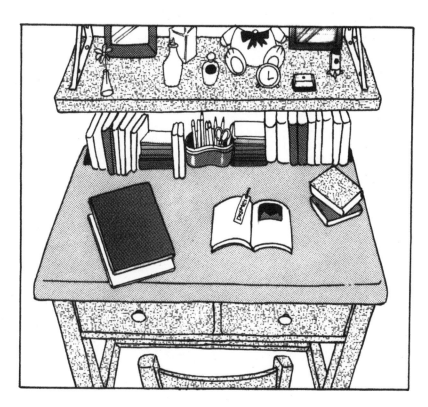

I use a heavy, wooden desk. It's a pretty basic design and doesn't come with shelves, so I special-ordered the shelf you see above the desk. Inside the drawer, I keep a diary and a 0.3 mm-nib pen, along with some other stuff. The pen is really useful because it allows me to write in really small lettering. I own the same kinds of things all girls own, but I still worry guys don't find me attractive.

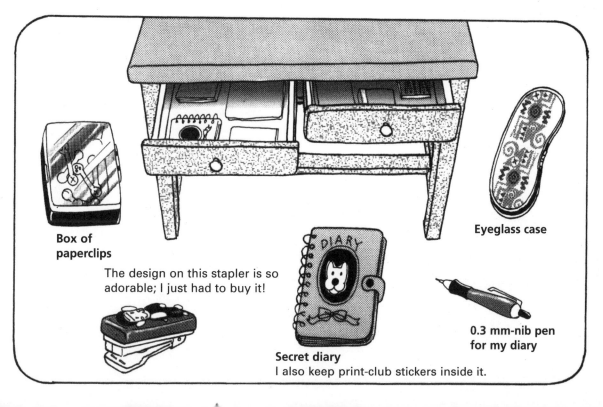

Box of paperclips

The design on this stapler is so adorable; I just had to buy it!

Secret diary
I also keep print-club stickers inside it.

Eyeglass case

0.3 mm-nib pen for my diary

Uppity Girl

The desk I use is large and has a built-in bookshelf. Underneath, is a set of drawers on casters giving me plenty of room for storage. Perhaps that's the reason I tend to keep things totally unrelated to school inside my desk drawers. I become tense easily, so I want to have incense and other stress-relievers around me.

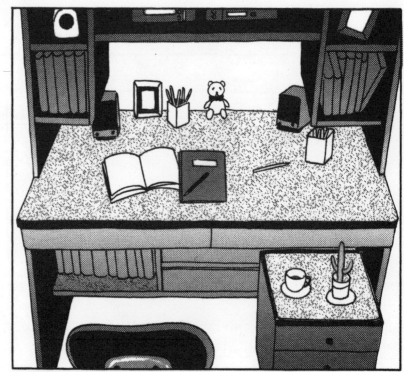

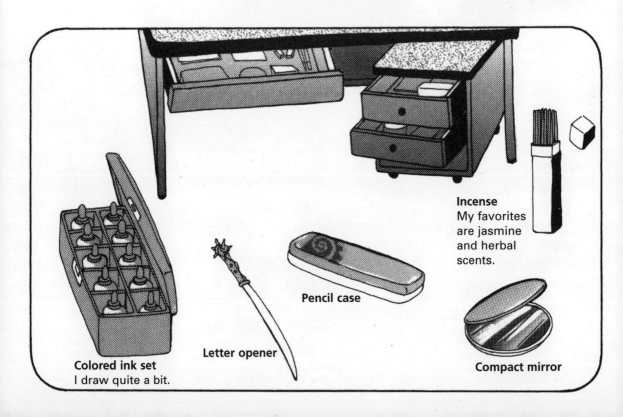

Colored ink set
I draw quite a bit.

Letter opener

Pencil case

Incense
My favorites are jasmine and herbal scents.

Compact mirror

❏ On the Balcony

Perky Girl

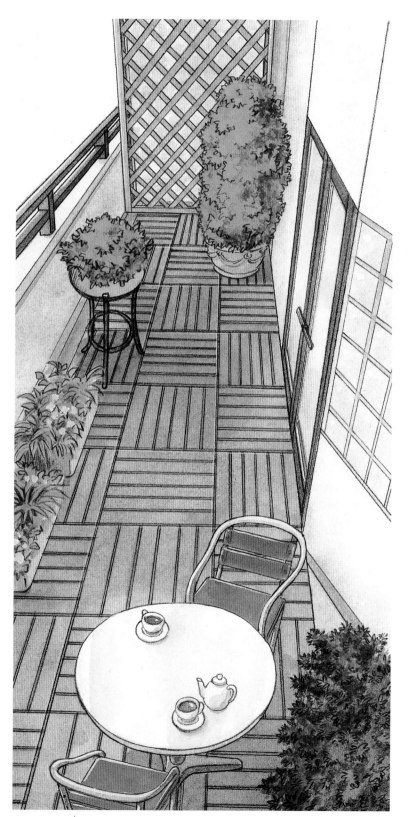

This is the typical balcony of a girl living on her own. There was enough room in the corner for me to put out a small table and chairs. I also set up planters to create a miniature garden. Isn't it absolutely perfect for inviting friends over for a snack or some tea when the weather is nice? At Christmas, I decorate the potted plants with ornaments and lights.

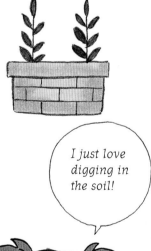

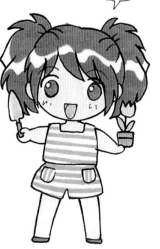

I just love digging in the soil!

Sporty Girl

My balcony is typical of the kind you find attached to a studio apartment. I laid down some artificial turf and put out a canvas patio chair. This is the perfect spot for sunbathing. I bought that storage chest you see in the corner at a shop specializing in self-assembly furniture and put it together myself. It was pretty easy.

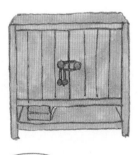

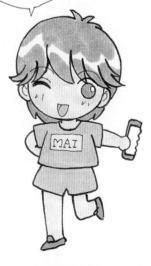

I enjoy assembling furniture!

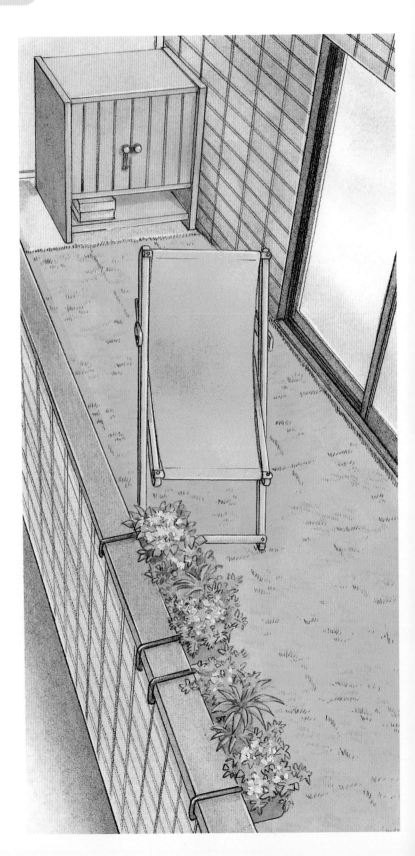

❏ *Around the Bed*

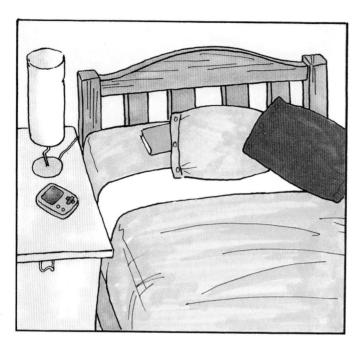

I don't have a nightstand, since it would just take up too much space in my already tiny studio. Instead, I use my desk for the same purpose. At night, I play video games or write in my diary (but only every now and then). I tend to hide my diary underneath my pillow.

Bed linens: My pillowcase is pink— my favorite color! My sheets are made of soft fibers, which I really like.

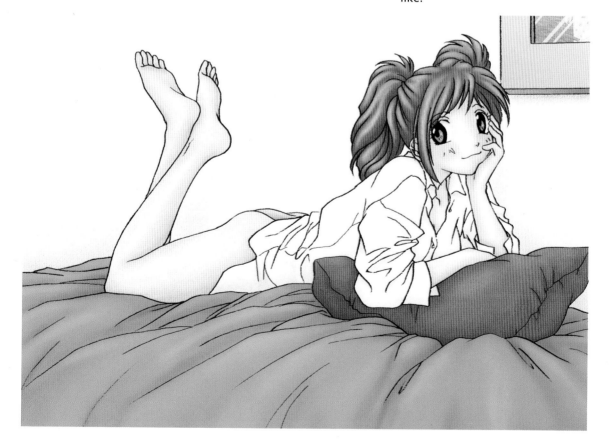

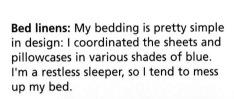

I sleep on an elevated bed, which allows me to store my television and other things underneath. I attached a small curio shelf to the wall just under the bed. I collect miniature chinaware, and display them on this shelf. It seems sort of empty though. I guess I'll have to add to my collection!

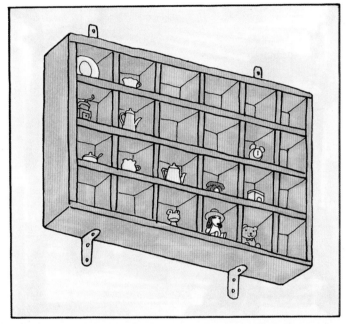

Bed linens: My bedding is pretty simple in design: I coordinated the sheets and pillowcases in various shades of blue. I'm a restless sleeper, so I tend to mess up my bed.

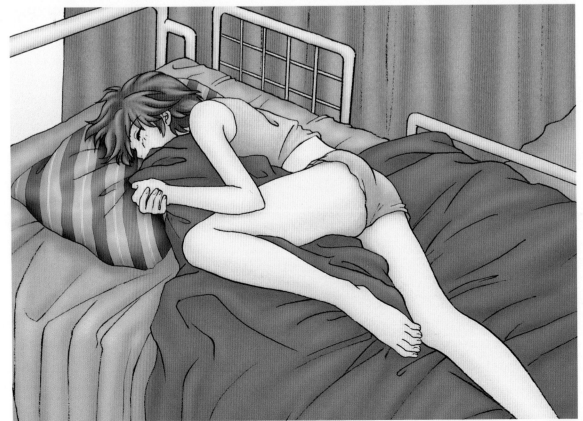

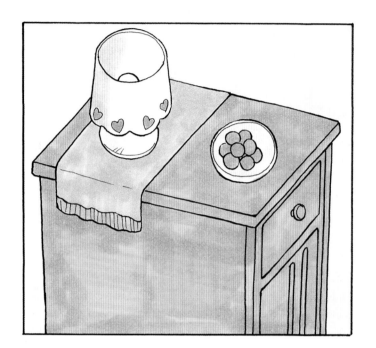

Dreamy Girl

I have a nightstand at the side of my bed. On top are a lamp and a bowl of cork with some potpourri I made myself. The potpourri is a mixture of lavender and herbs. When I'm lying in my bed, the aroma wafts over me and puts me in a tranquil mood. Unfortunately, I think the potpourri makes me a little too relaxed, because I have a tendency to oversleep.

Bed linens: I have a really frilly pillowcase, and my sheets are all various shades of pink. My comforter is made of a really smooth, satiny fabric, which feels great against my skin.

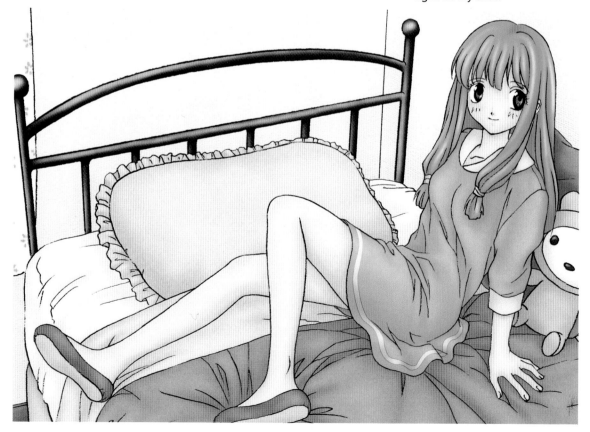

Precocious Girl

At the head of my bed, I keep a trunk where I store linens. It's really handy.

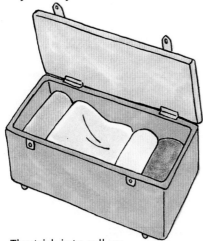

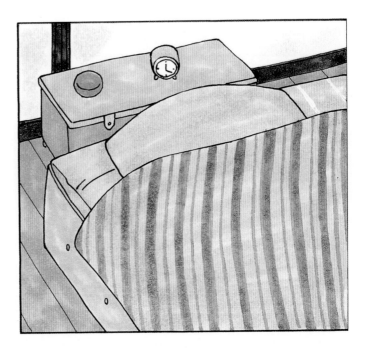

The trick is to roll up the linens tightly, so they can be packed closely together.

Bed linens: I used a king-sized pillow. I went with a subdued color scheme because I thought it would be more calming.

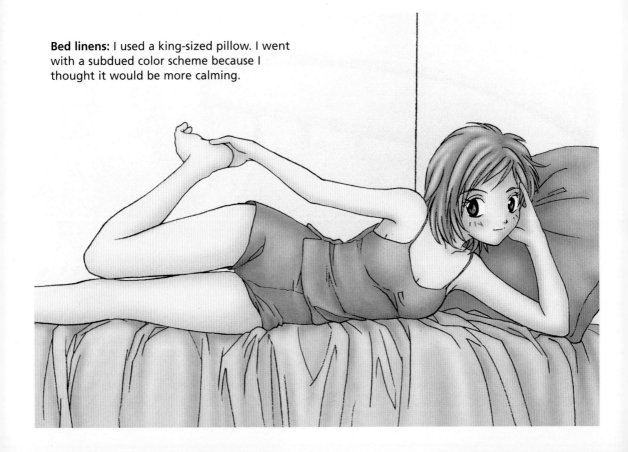

Shy Girl

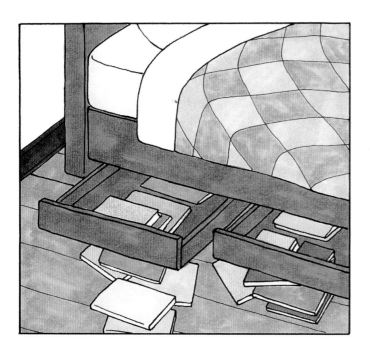

My bed has drawers underneath. I had intended on storing my sheets in these drawers, but since I like to read in bed, they ended up being full of books instead... I try to keep my books organized, but they just seem to increase faster than I can control, so they're always mixed up.

Bed linens: I have a sturdy wood-frame bed, so I tried to coordinate my sheets with greens and forest-type colors. Every morning, I make my bed carefully, tucking the bedspread around the pillows.

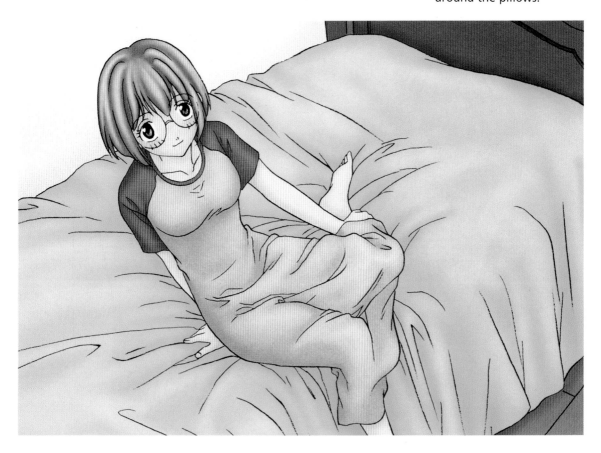

Uppity Girl

I have an elegant nightstand at the side of my bed, minimally decorated with a single lamp. I keep novels and small items articles in the drawer. I like to keep a handkerchief or small cloth under the lamp, and tend to change the cloth according to my mood. I fall asleep pretty easily, so I don't read in bed very often.

Bed linens: Most of my sheets are a clean, crisp white. I change my sheets pretty regularly, so I have two or three matching sets. I also bought a few red pillowcases because I heard red has a cheering effect.

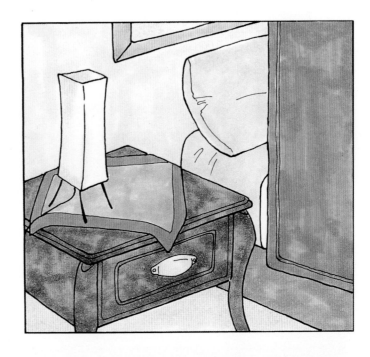

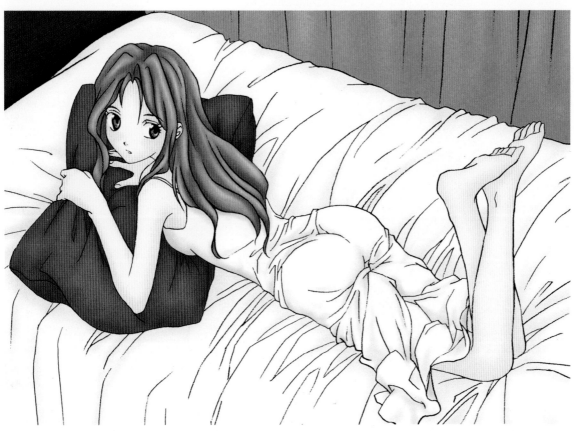

➡ **Bath Time**

Perky Girl

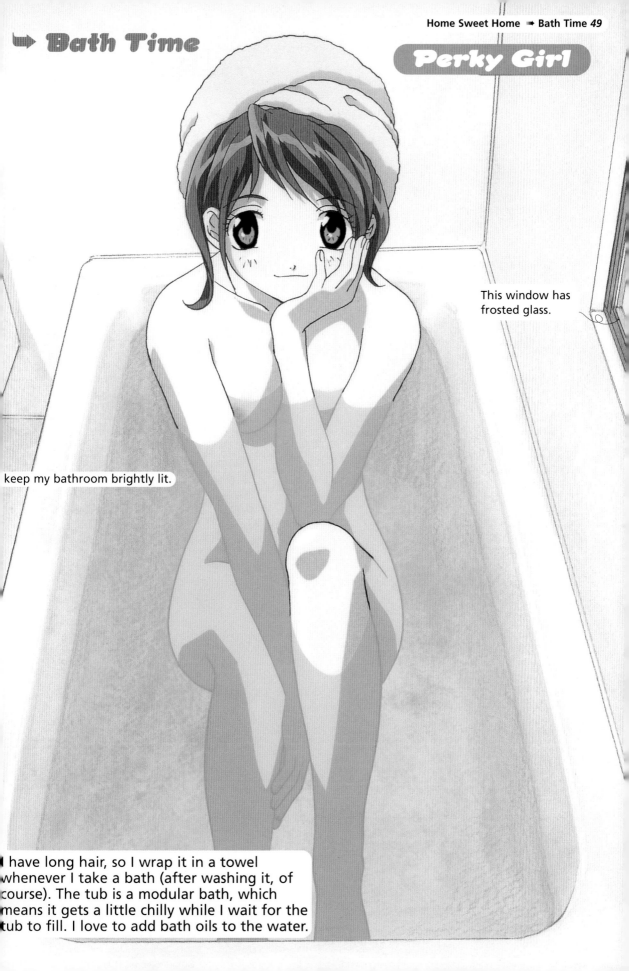

This window has frosted glass.

keep my bathroom brightly lit.

I have long hair, so I wrap it in a towel whenever I take a bath (after washing it, of course). The tub is a modular bath, which means it gets a little chilly while I wait for the tub to fill. I love to add bath oils to the water.

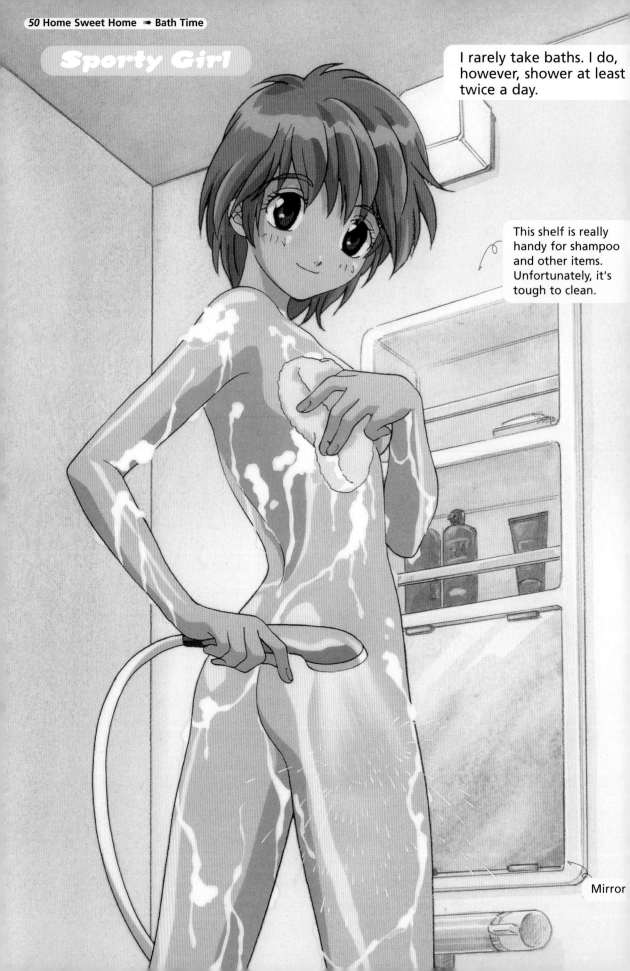

My hair is delicate and easily damaged, so I take extra care in selecting my shampoo. I wrap my hair in a steaming, hot towel while I soak in the bath. Naturally, I use a different shampoo and conditioner from the rest of my family.

Dreamy Girl

I take a bunch of hair in my hand and rinse it carefully, bit by bit.

We have a large mirror in our bathroom, which is really terrific. It's set so that it won't cloud.

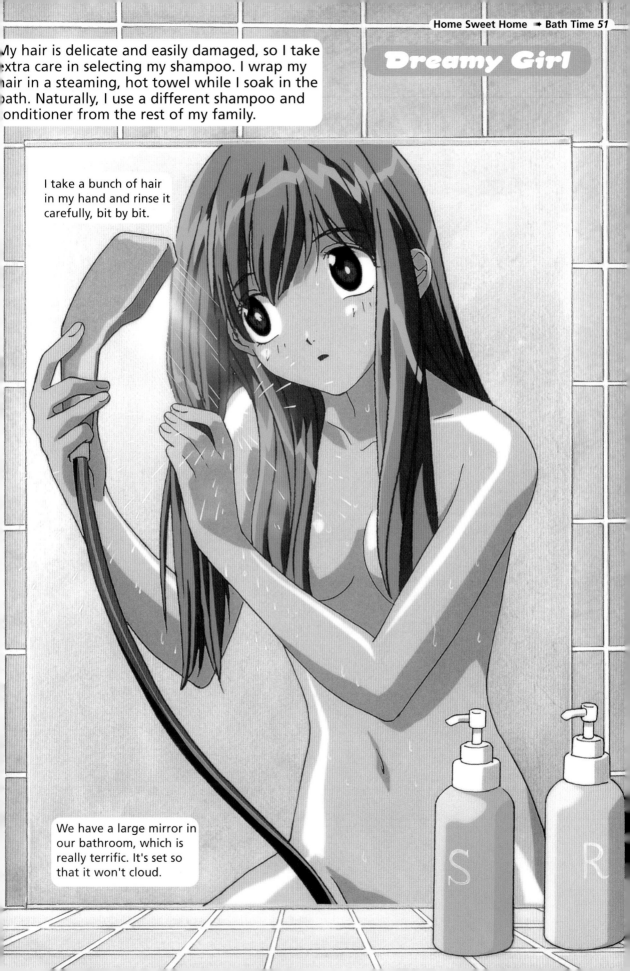

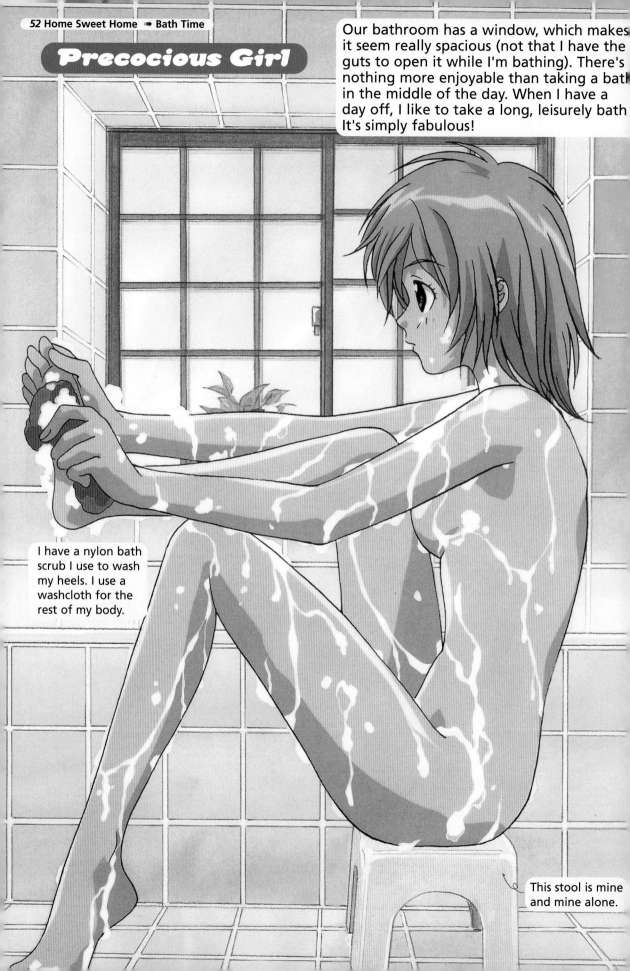

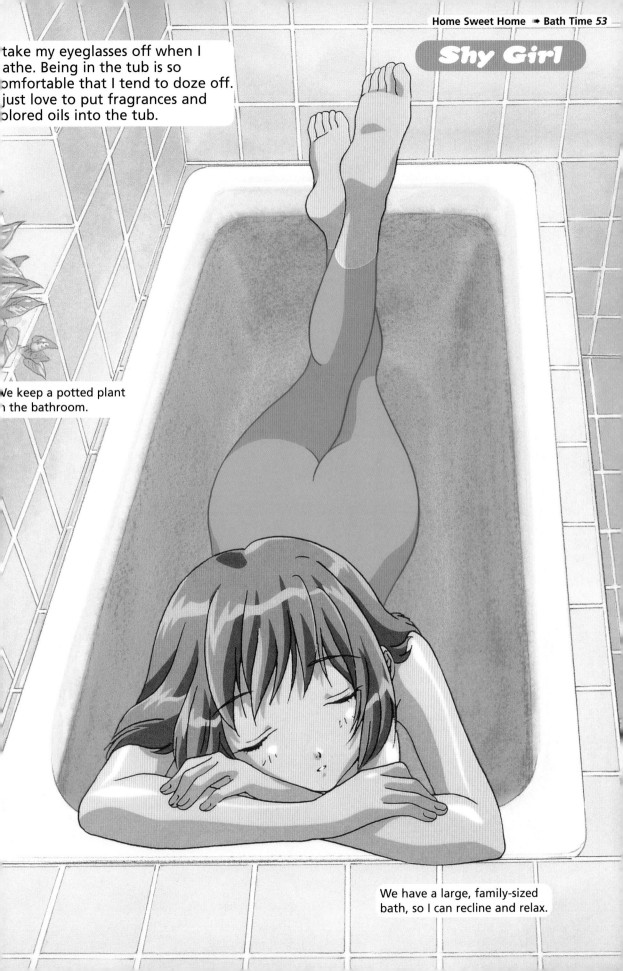

Shy Girl

take my eyeglasses off when I
bathe. Being in the tub is so
comfortable that I tend to doze off.
I just love to put fragrances and
colored oils into the tub.

We keep a potted plant
in the bathroom.

We have a large, family-sized
bath, so I can recline and relax.

Uppity Girl

Our bathroom is paneled in Japanese cypress, which gives off a wonderful, relaxing aroma. I tend to spend a while in the bath and use the time to do some stretching.

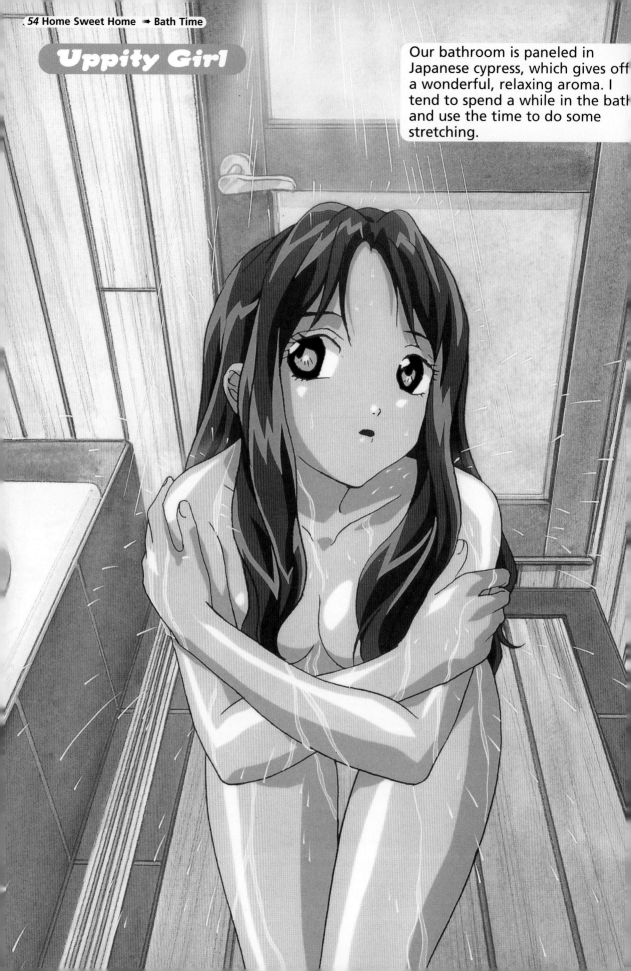

Basic Character Design II

There are many definitions of what constitutes a bishoujo (pretty young girl). I came up with the following 10 points based on the characters appearing in this book. Ideally, you should draw the type of character you personally find pretty. However, if you find yourself at a loss when it comes time to put pen to paper, go ahead and use these 10 points as reference.

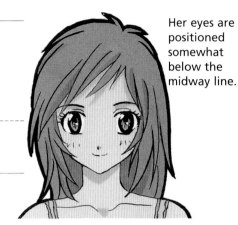

Her eyes are positioned somewhat below the midway line.

1. The height should be 6 to 7 heads in length.

Anything less than this would make your character appear childish, while anything more would make her appear too mature.

2. Aim for a childish face.

Specifically, the eyes should be positioned about midway on the face, the eyes should be taller than wide, and the cheeks should be full.

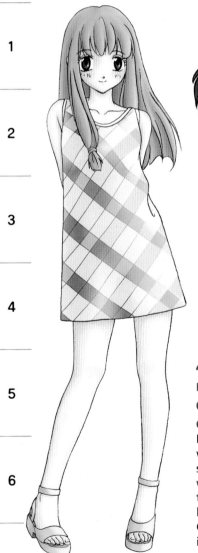

1

2

3

4

5

6

Omit the ribs!

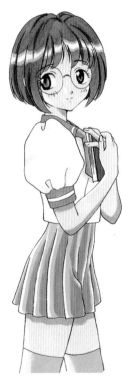

4. Avoid adding too many lines when drawing the character nude.

Drawing your character with too many lines to suggest bones and muscles will make her seem a little too real and cause her to lose her girlish suppleness. Create your character by imagining a girl with delicate bones and soft flesh.

3. It is important to select a body type that works well with a school uniform.

Since these characters are still in school, they should have the body type of an adolescent girl who has not fully matured. Making the character's breasts too large or giving her too many curves will make her seem like she has a costume fetish if she is drawn in a school uniform.

5. Do bangs make the character more appealing?

This depends on the character. However, adding bangs to a character rather than showing her wearing her hair tied in a bun will prevent her from appearing too mature.

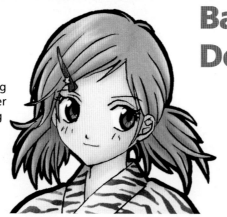

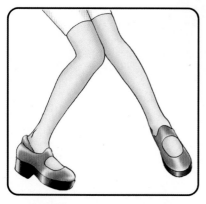

6. Keep the skin color light.

Naturally, this does not mean you should draw your character with completely white skin. Some characters look adorable with tanned skin, but only give her truly dark skin if it matches her ethnicity. Otherwise, she will appear like the victim of a tanning booth.

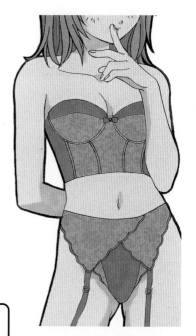

7. Avoid overly narrow ankles.

Again, this depends on the character. However, giving her a little flesh will make her seem more girlish than drawing her with the clearly defined tendons of a trim woman's ankle.

8. Simplify the nails.

Drawing the line where nail meets the cuticle will suffice. Any more detail will make the hand appear too lifelike.

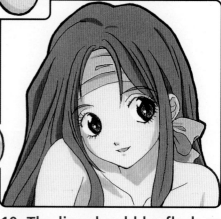

9. Avoid realistic shading.

Especially when drawing a bare bottom or stomach! Shading could potentially make your character's flesh appear to be sagging. Draw her with smooth, firm flesh.

10. The lips should be flesh or pale pink.

Keep the contours small, delicate and cute.

Girly Stuff

Chapter 2

Inside the Schoolbag (Briefcase type)

This is a typical schoolbag. Such bags are usually made of genuine or imitation leather. They are easy to carry but quite heavy when packed. Schoolgirls carry lots of things around with them. Common schoolbag contents include an album for print-club stickers, makeup, fashion accessories, and textbooks, of course. Each school has different rules as to what students are allowed to have with them; here is list of items that are usually acceptable.

Album for print-club stickers
Girls carry these around everywhere.

Uni-Posca paint marker for writing messages.

POSCA

A pack of tissues and a handkerchief in the front pocket

Girls like to decorate their bags with character keychains.

Toothbrush and toothpaste
A girl likes to brush after lunc

Sock Touch
Roll on glue to hold up socks.

Hairbrush

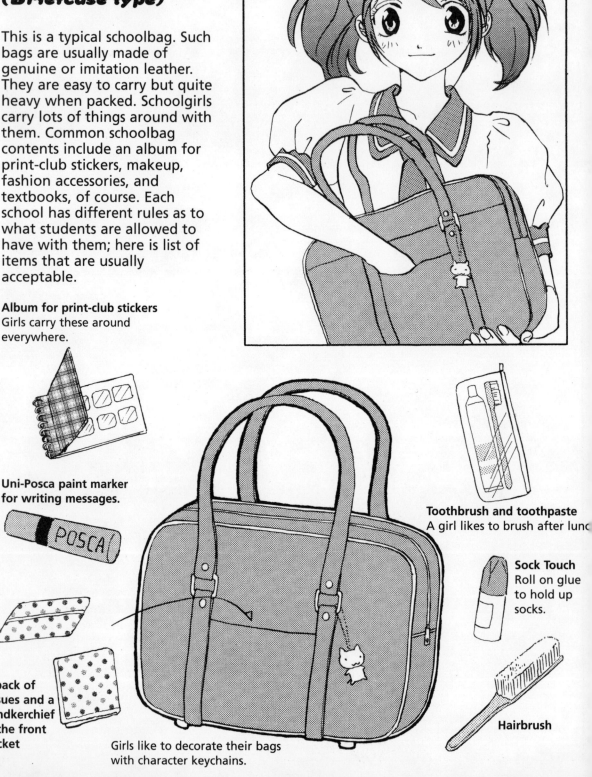

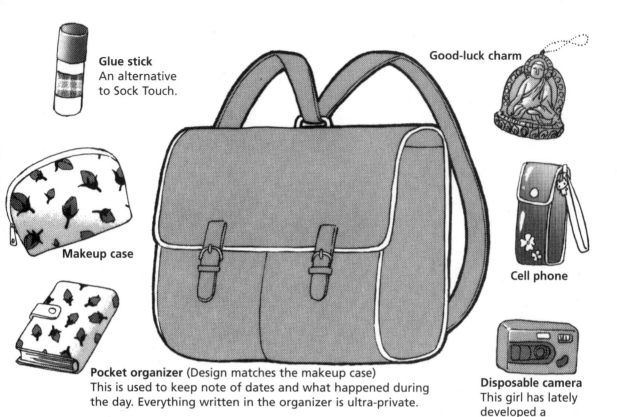

Glue stick
An alternative to Sock Touch.

Good-luck charm

Makeup case

Cell phone

Pocket organizer (Design matches the makeup case)
This is used to keep note of dates and what happened during the day. Everything written in the organizer is ultra-private.

Disposable camera
This girl has lately developed a passion for taking snapshots.

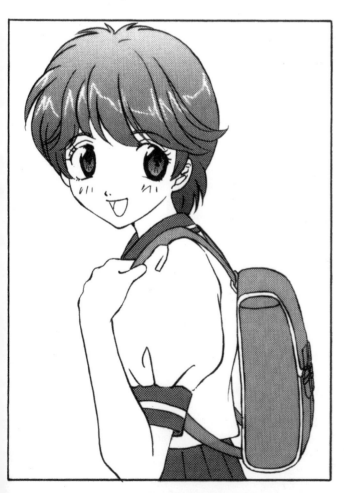

Inside the Schoolbag
(Backpack type)

A backpack is terrific for when it rains or when a girl has a lot to carry. This backpack is made of canvas, so care must be taken not to pack in too much or it will lose its shape. Most school backpacks come in dark colors: navy blue, brown and forest green. Inside are a cell phone, a disposable camera, a makeup case and an assortment of other necessities.

Crystal Balls & Good-Luck Charms

Girls have a whole host of concerns, so it is only natural that they would develop an interest in fortunetelling. There are many different styles of fortunetelling, ranging from current fads such as Feng Shui to tarot-card reading to astrology. On these pages are presented an assortment of fortunetelling styles as well as such good-luck charms as amulets and talismans.

The Crystal Ball

Because crystal ball-gazing is guided by the power of meditation, the practice often is accompanied by the burning of candles and incense to relax the mind of the diviner. Most young women visit a fortuneteller rather than attempt divination on their own.

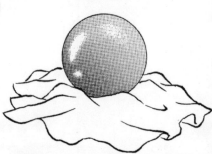

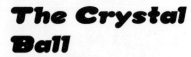

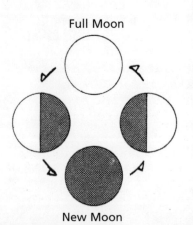

Full Moon

New Moon

Moon Phase Divination

This involves prognostication based on the lunar cycle. The belief that the moon's phases influence our behavior has led to attention being paid to its cycle. Reading the current phase of the moon is believed to provide insight to one's psychological state for that day. This style of fortunetelling appears regularly in Japanese women's magazines.

This is an amulet containing a blessed grain of rice. The amulet is supposedly filled with life force and brings good fortune.

Encased blessed rice grain

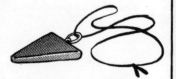

This pendant is a power stone, which believers claim can awaken the subconscious.

This steel-gray stone, whose name was derived from the ancient Greek for "blood," is supposed to cleanse the blood, condition the body and bring good luck. It is an optimal item for girls who always feel chilly and are looking to improve their blood circulation.

Said to possess a "blue spiritual light," larimar is believed to have the ability to beckon encounters. A necklace with a larimar pendant is thought to improve interpersonal relationships, while a larimar ring, when worn on the ring finger of the right hand, is said to help attract a romantic partner.

Aventurine, a good-luck talisman, is believed to help transform luck from yin to yang. Aventurine works well when worn to fulfill an earnest wish or dream.

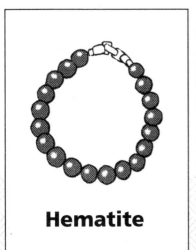

Hematite

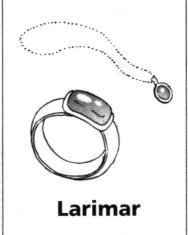

Larimar

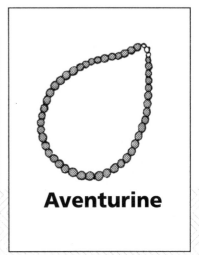

Aventurine

Power Stones and Other Talismans: Beckoning Good Fortune

Star Rose Quartz

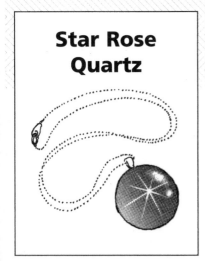

Blue Calcite

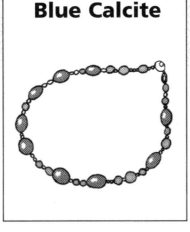

Angel Quartz

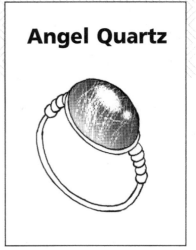

Possessing both powers of love and beauty, when this stone is held up to light, it appears to have a glittering star in its core. It is said to guide your destined partner to you, so it is perfect for those looking for that significant other.

A type of marble, this stone is characterized by its appearance of having multiple layers of crystal. Blue calcite is thought to eliminate excess energy, facilitating one's ability to make reasonable decisions and improving one's memory.

This stone, believed to possess the power to maximize one's life force and vitality, appears to have encased within it strands of rutile. Angel quartz is recommended for dispelling depression or melancholy.

A Peek into the Jewelry Box
Necklaces and Bracelets

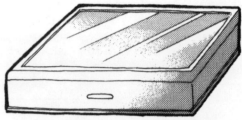

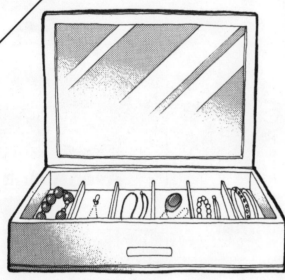

This jewelry box is designed to store necklaces, but it functions just as well holding bracelets. The box itself is made of wood, while the lid is glass, making it easy for a girl to make her choice.   There are five or six dividers inside, and each compartment can hold two or three necklaces and bracelets. Keeping too many in one compartment results in the necklaces and bracelets tangling, which is an absolute grief to undo. To prevent tarnishing, the necklaces and bracelets need to be carefully cleaned before being put away.

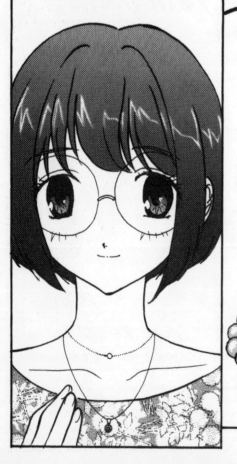

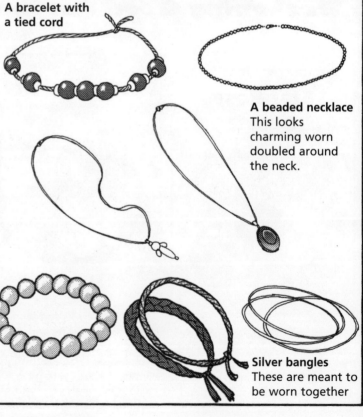

A bracelet with a tied cord

A beaded necklace
This looks charming worn doubled around the neck.

Silver bangles
These are meant to be worn together

A Peek into the Jewelry Box
Earrings and Rings

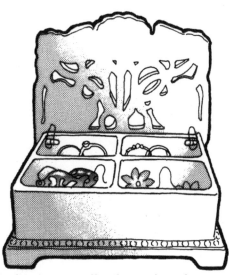

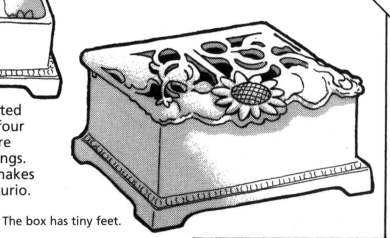

This is a small, silver-plated jewelry box. Inside are four compartments, which are perfect for storing earrings. The design of the box makes it a nice decoration or curio.

The box has tiny feet.

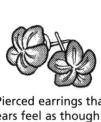

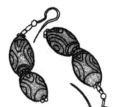

Pierced earrings that are too large make your ears feel as though they are being pulled down.

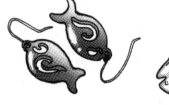
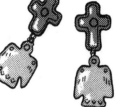

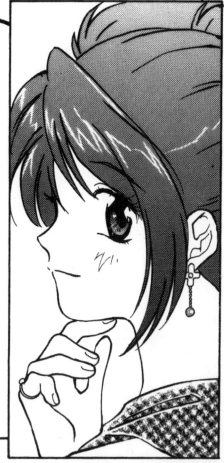

Hair Accessory Case

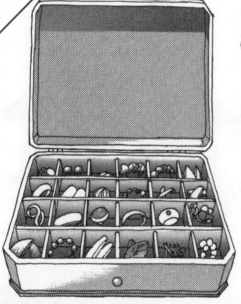

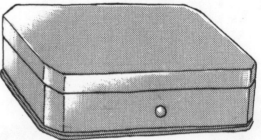

This is a light and colorful plastic case. The interior is divided into numerous small compartments, so that each barrette or hairpin set occupies a separate section. The interior is shallow, allowing for easy retrieval of the items stored.

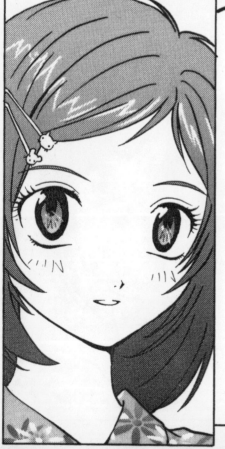

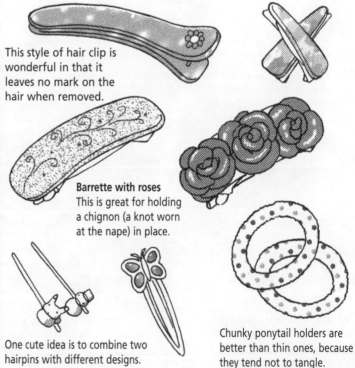

This style of hair clip is wonderful in that it leaves no mark on the hair when removed.

Barrette with roses
This is great for holding a chignon (a knot worn at the nape) in place.

One cute idea is to combine two hairpins with different designs.

Chunky ponytail holders are better than thin ones, because they tend not to tangle.

Here are a few wild-animal patterns for the untamed girl. Select your favorite. These designs go well with leather fashions.

Flower and animal decals dress up these phones. Decorate your own to match the season.

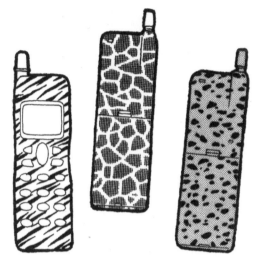
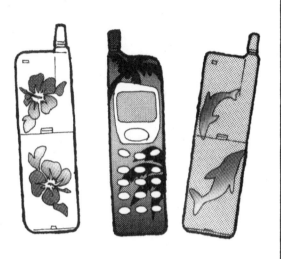

Stylish Cell Phones

Cell phone accessories and decorative patterns are all the rage in Japan. There are so many choices, it is hard to know where to begin. Only a small sample is presented on this page. However, new styles are constantly appearing, so it's a good idea for a girl to go window shopping to get an idea of what's available. It seems now like the trend is leaning toward straps for suspending the cell phone from the neck. Try your hand at making your own.

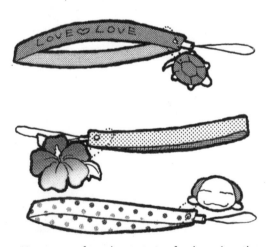
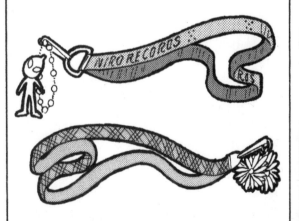

Here are a few short straps for hanging the phone from a schoolbag or tote. They are inexpensive and come in a wide assortment of designs, making it great fun to choose. They can also double as camera straps, provided the camera is compact and light.

These longer straps are for hanging the phone from the neck. They come in fabrics as well as leather, and can double as a keychain.

Day trip

Makeup case

Fan
Not necessary for winter trips

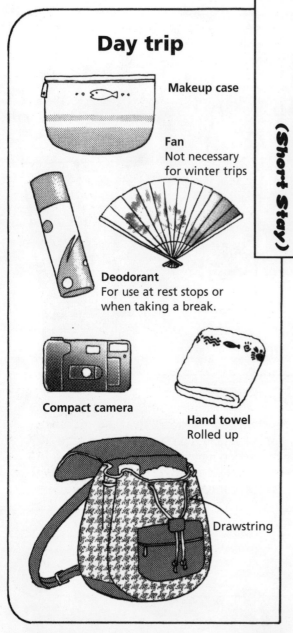

Deodorant
For use at rest stops or when taking a break.

Compact camera

Hand towel
Rolled up

Drawstring

Overnight Stay

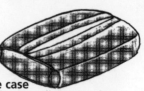

Floral-pattern bath towel

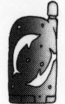

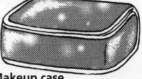

Tissue case
Inside is a complimentary tissue pack. [Note: In Japan, complimentary tissue packs are distributed as a form of advertising.]

Cell phone
This one is decorated for the summer.

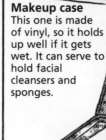

Makeup case
This one is made of vinyl, so it holds up well if it gets wet. It can serve to hold facial cleansers and sponges.

This travel case is packed with a sketchbook and some stationery.

This is how the case looks opened.

A small wicker travel case that allows for ventilation is ideal for overnight stays. It is stylish and lightweight. What could be better? If you do not intend on staying at a hotel, be sure to bring a bath towel. An oversized T-shirt is a popular alternative to pajamas or a nightgown. A fabric backpack serves well for day trips. A fan and a hand towel are vital.

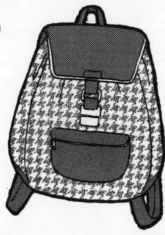

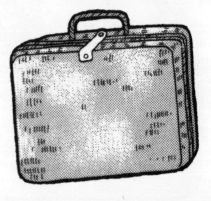

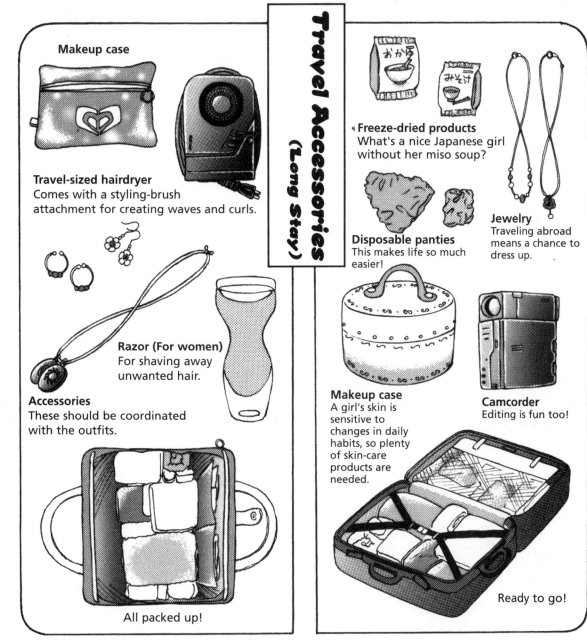

Travel Accessories (Long Stay)

Makeup case

Travel-sized hairdryer
Comes with a styling-brush attachment for creating waves and curls.

Razor (For women)
For shaving away unwanted hair.

Accessories
These should be coordinated with the outfits.

All packed up!

◄ Freeze-dried products
What's a nice Japanese girl without her miso soup?

Disposable panties
This makes life so much easier!

Jewelry
Traveling abroad means a chance to dress up.

Makeup case
A girl's skin is sensitive to changes in daily habits, so plenty of skin-care products are needed.

Camcorder
Editing is fun too!

Ready to go!

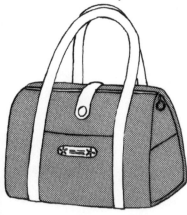

A leather bag in and of itself can be rather heavy.

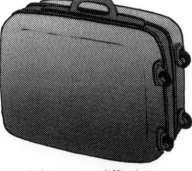

Suitcases are difficult to maneuver on stairs.

A hairdryer and assorted jewelry and accessories should be brought on domestic trips that last two or more nights. Few Japanese hotels and traditional-style inns provide curling irons or brushes. The travel case should also be somewhat larger than that used for a single-night stay. Overseas trips usually involve a four- to seven-night stay, which calls for a suitcase. This should be roomy enough to pack oodles of souvenirs. Wheeled suitcases are surprisingly maneuverable.

Beach Gear

Beach sandals

Bikini

Suntan oil

Sunglasses

Terrycloth poncho
This can be used even after changing out of the bathing suit.

How to Wear a Paleo (bathing sarong)

① Open the paleo behind you, holding one side in each hand.

② Wrap the two sides around the front, looping the top with a simple knot.

③ Tie the ends around the back of your neck, adjusting the paleo to a suitable length.

This is how it should look.

What is a paleo?

A paleo is a large colorful cloth wrapped around the body and worn over a bathing suit. Paleos are very versatile and can also be laid on the sand and used in place of a beach towel.

Winter Sports

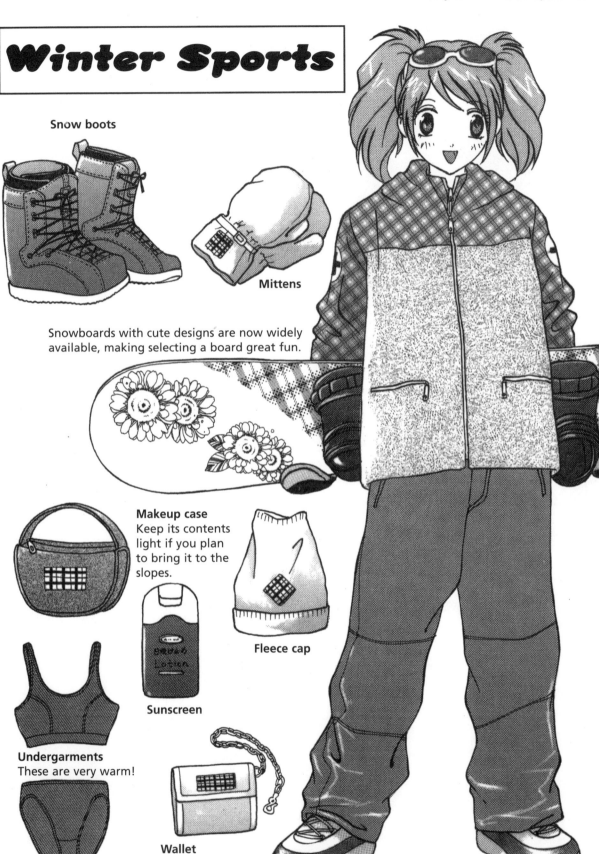

Snow boots

Mittens

Snowboards with cute designs are now widely available, making selecting a board great fun.

Makeup case
Keep its contents light if you plan to bring it to the slopes.

Fleece cap

Sunscreen

Undergarments
These are very warm!

Wallet
The chain allows it to be attached to a belt.

Inside the Makeup Case

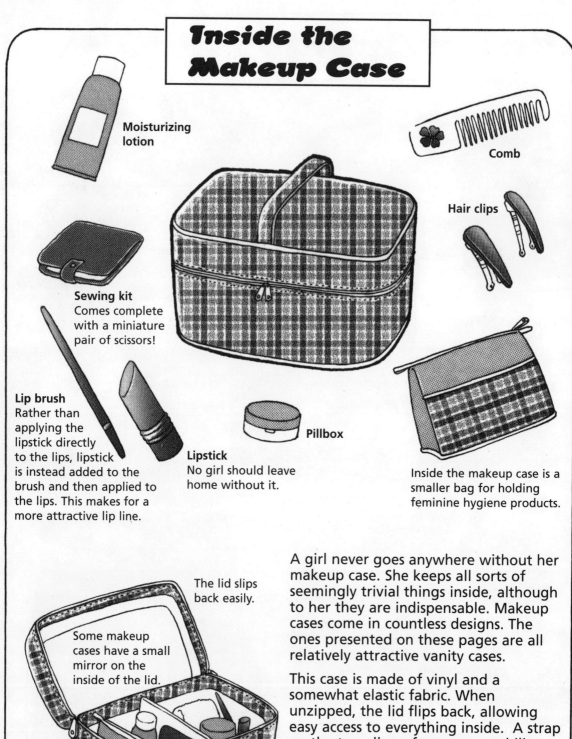

Moisturizing lotion

Comb

Hair clips

Sewing kit
Comes complete with a miniature pair of scissors!

Lip brush
Rather than applying the lipstick directly to the lips, lipstick is instead added to the brush and then applied to the lips. This makes for a more attractive lip line.

Lipstick
No girl should leave home without it.

Pillbox

Inside the makeup case is a smaller bag for holding feminine hygiene products.

The lid slips back easily.

Some makeup cases have a small mirror on the inside of the lid.

A girl never goes anywhere without her makeup case. She keeps all sorts of seemingly trivial things inside, although to her they are indispensable. Makeup cases come in countless designs. The ones presented on these pages are all relatively attractive vanity cases.

This case is made of vinyl and a somewhat elastic fabric. When unzipped, the lid flips back, allowing easy access to everything inside. A strap on the top allows for easy portability. The interior is subdivided into several compartments, and the case itself is tall enough to allow travel-size cosmetic bottles to be stored upright. This means the contents are fully visible and there is no need for concern about spilling or leaking.

Inside the Makeup Case

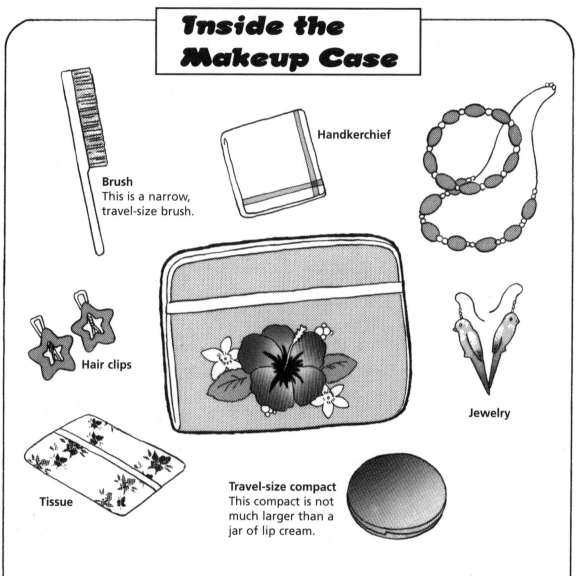

Brush
This is a narrow, travel-size brush.

Handkerchief

Hair clips

Jewelry

Tissue

Travel-size compact
This compact is not much larger than a jar of lip cream.

The exterior of this makeup case features an ornate hibiscus flower design. It is folded like a wallet and has a zipper. Items are extremely easy to access, since the case can be opened and laid flat. However, its slim design prevents it from being able to hold bottles and jars. Inside are pockets for holding lip and eyebrow pencils and the like, making organizing the contents a snap. A large inside pocket with a zipper holds jewelry and other accessories. Since it is small and light, it can be slipped easily into a handbag.

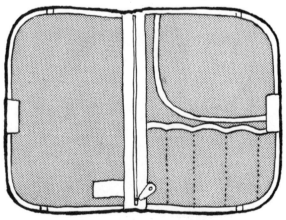

The case fully opened

Dieting

"If only I could wear a miniskirt." "I wish my arms were slender enough that I could wear a tank top or camisole." "I just don't have the courage to wear something that leaves my navel exposed." It takes a surprising amount of effort for girls to squeeze themselves into the latest and most desirable fashions. Young women feel very strongly about their physical appearance. Some are even afraid of gaining a mere quarter-pound. Yet, young women's bodies are still growing, and it is no easy feat to suppress an appetite. Diets are a constant topic.

Slimming Down

Pulse meter

Body Refining Gel

Massage oil

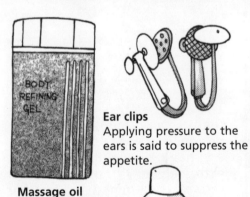

Ear clips
Applying pressure to the ears is said to suppress the appetite.

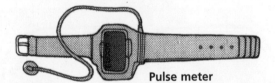

Toy "diet pig"
Dissuade overeating.

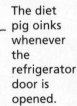

The diet pig oinks whenever the refrigerator door is opened.

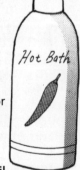

Hot Bath

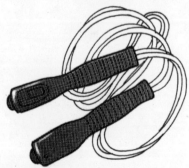

Jump-rope and electronic jump counter
The counter indicates the number of skips.

Hot chili pepper bath oil
Hot chili peppers increase the metabolic rate, raising the amount of calories burned.

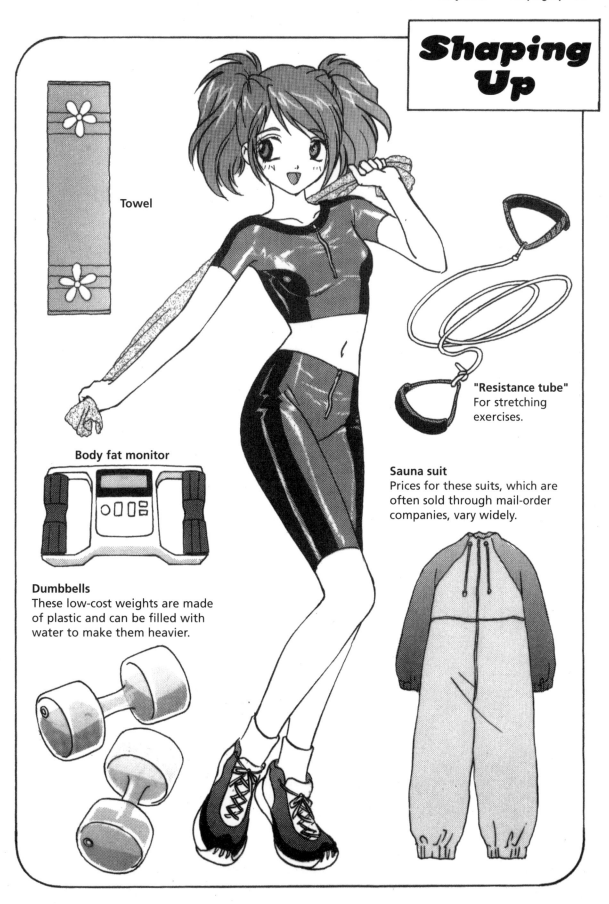

Shaping Up

Towel

"Resistance tube"
For stretching exercises.

Body fat monitor

Sauna suit
Prices for these suits, which are often sold through mail-order companies, vary widely.

Dumbbells
These low-cost weights are made of plastic and can be filled with water to make them heavier.

Health Products

Cosmetics alone will not make a girl pretty. However, maintaining a properly balanced diet will ensure that you are beautiful on the inside as well as out. Women's magazines carry special features on diets two or three times a year. Young women with a keen interest in eating properly and looking good do lots of research to learn which products are best.

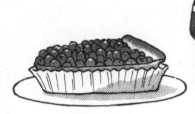

Blueberry pie

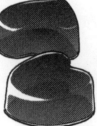

Pomegranate gelatin

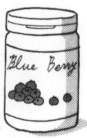

Blueberry tablets

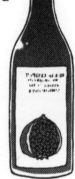

Pomegranate juice

The above are a few of the pomegranate and blueberry foodstuffs now enjoying popularity. Pomegranate, which has the ability to maintain regularity in hormonal secretions, is selling well among young women. Blueberry contains properties that improve eyesight. Whether in pie or gelatin form, blueberry tastes delicious, so young women can look good and enjoy their diets at the same time.

Tea

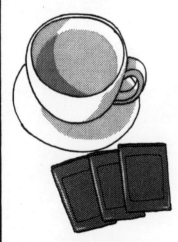

Green tea contains lots of vitamins, but sometimes a girl needs a little variety at snack time. A Chinese tea made with rose leaves is terrific for conditioning the skin, while tea made with garcinia is great for those on a diet. Of course, choosing the right teacup to drink from is equally important!

Energy bars

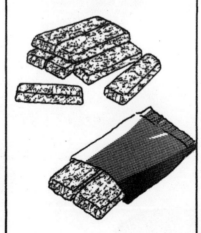

Energy bars are handy for a girl on the run. These products, which essentially taste like cookies, come fortified with vitamins and are low in calories. They make an optimal alternative to traditional snack foods, plus their high fiber content helps ensure regularity. Favorite flavors include chocolate, creamery butter and French toast.

Supplements

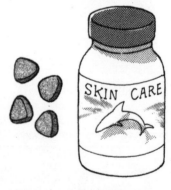

These may not be all that fun going down, but they seem to be effective. One popular supplement contains chondroitin, a substance said to be good for maintaining the skin's moisture and found in abundance in sharks' fins. Other products include supplements providing the recommended daily amounts of vitamins and minerals. Naturally, this does not preclude eating properly.

Skin Care

Attractive young women are known for their dewy, supple skin. Skill in applying cosmetics is important, but even more critical is ensuring that the skin underneath is well toned. The following pages present the basics of skin care.

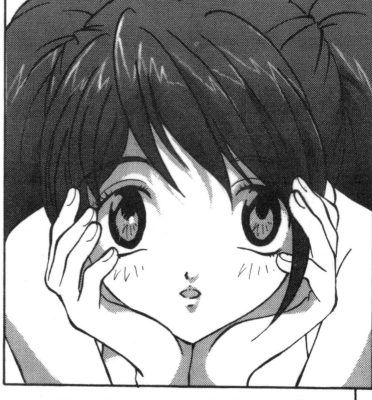

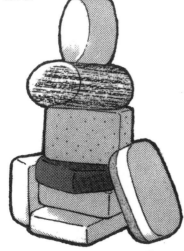

There are a wide variety of soaps on the market, and it can be difficult finding one that matches your skin type.

Skin-lightening Cosmetics

A large number of skin-lightening cosmetics (which remove soiling and discoloring of the skin, leaving the skin glowing and white) have recently been appearing in stores. A girl has to be diligent about controlling freckles and spots resulting from exposure to the sun.

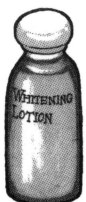

Toners
Toners are first applied to a cotton pad or ball and then lightly daubed on the skin.

Facial cleansing lotions
Apply, then rinse away with water and you're done!

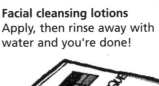

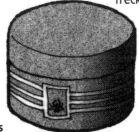

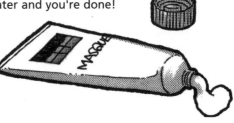

Creams
For best results, spread the cream over the skin like a facial pack and then apply a steaming hot towel.

The ABC's of Skin Care

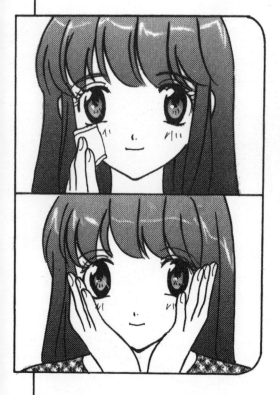

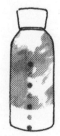

① After washing the face, toner is applied to a cotton or gauze pad and daubed on the skin. The key is to apply a large volume to the skin and allow it to absorb thoroughly. Those with acne may opt for medicated lotions or astringents. Those with sensitive skin tend to go for mild liquids with no additives.

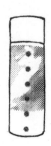

② Next comes the milk lotion. A bit is poured into the hands, and then the face is cupped and the lotion applied in a patting motion. Milk lotion has much more liquid consistency than it appears (at first glance it appears to have the consistency of a moisturizing lotion), so it does not leave a sticky residue, even if applied excessively. When the skin is in good condition, it is safe to skip the next steps.

③ When the skin is particularly dry, such as in winter, cream is applied to moisturize the skin. The cream is applied to a cotton ball or pad and spread evenly over the face. Moisturizing cream is especially effective when applied at night, leaving the face well hydrated in the morning.

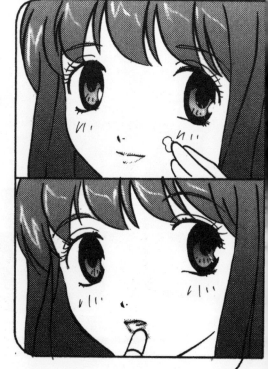

④ Last come the lips. Lips tend to become chapped from removing lipstick or cracked from dryness in the air. A girl has to put effort into caring for her lips. Most people are familiar with lip balm products for use by both men and women, but women tend to be pickier about what they use. Balms containing herbal essences and others with yummy, all-natural scents, such as vanilla, are the most popular.

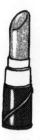

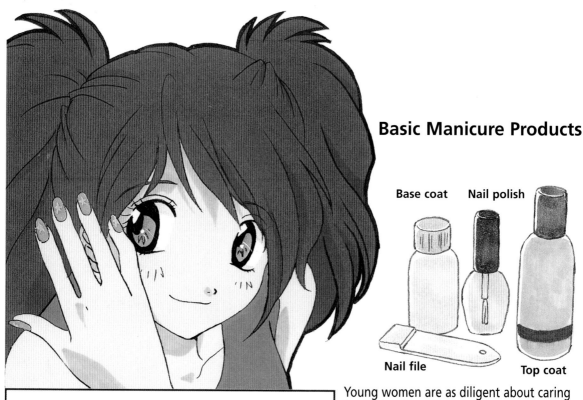

Basic Manicure Products

Base coat Nail polish

Nail file Top coat

Manicures

Young women are as diligent about caring for their nails as they are about taking care of their skin and makeup. Truth be told, lacquers are bad for the nails. This means that the nails require proper care after the polish is removed, or else they will dry out.

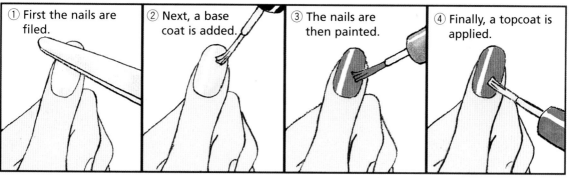

① First the nails are filed.

② Next, a base coat is added.

③ The nails are then painted.

④ Finally, a topcoat is applied.

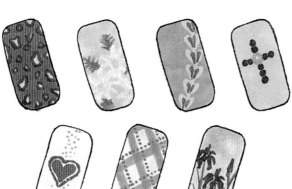

Artificial Nails

Young women whose nails tend to break or who experience difficulties growing their nails may opt for artificial nails. They come in a variety of shapes and lengths and are convenient in that they tend to last longer than nail polish. Nail art is also enjoying popularity, and girls who are skilled at it have exquisite nails with complex designs enhanced with rhinestones and glitter.

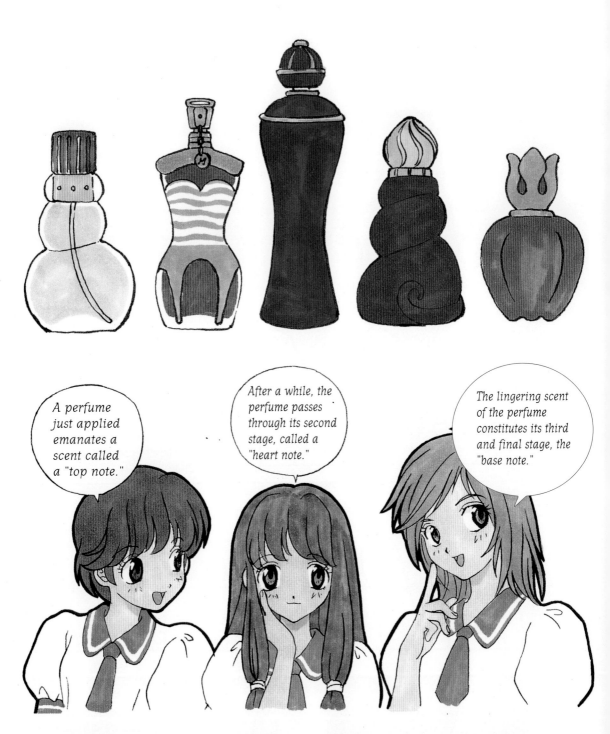

A perfume just applied emanates a scent called a "top note."

After a while, the perfume passes through its second stage, called a "heart note."

The lingering scent of the perfume constitutes its third and final stage, the "base note."

Perfumes

Perfumes are something that interest all girls without fail and come in a wide range, from sweet floral scents to spicy herbal scents. Many perfumes found in stores are sold not as cosmetics but for aromatherapy to assist relaxation. Classes are also now being taught on how to blend one's own special fragrances.

Applying Perfume Naturally, perfume is not applied directly to the face. Normally, it is sprayed using an atomizer. One or two spritzes are applied to the wrists, nape of the neck, or other areas close to a pulse, which causes the cologne to evaporate and disperse in the air.

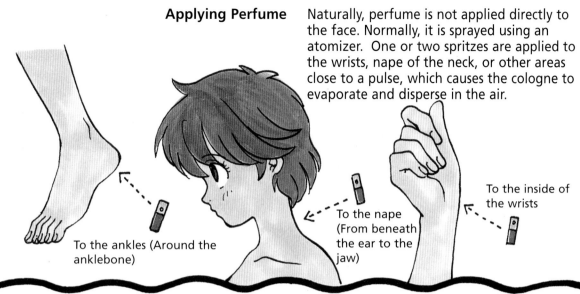

To the ankles (Around the anklebone)

To the nape (From beneath the ear to the jaw)

To the inside of the wrists

An "aroma bear" is a fragranced teddy bear. A "fragrance gel" is a shimmering, clear gel that is absolutely scrumptious and which is rubbed directly onto the skin. Bottled perfumes have applicators attached to their lids, which are dipped into the perfume and then applied to the skin.

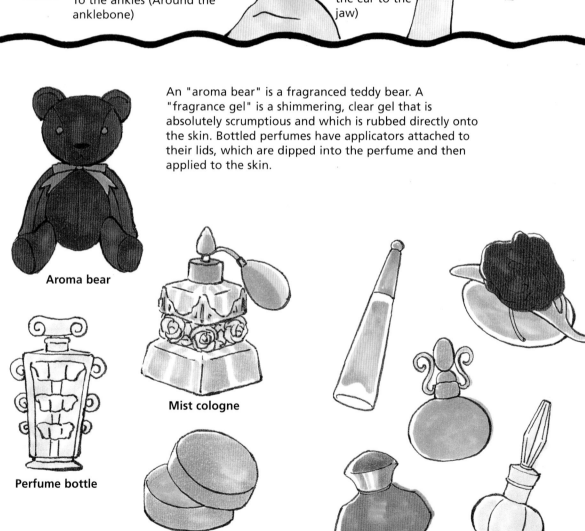

Aroma bear

Perfume bottle

Mist cologne

Fragrance gel gels

It is not only the fragrances themselves that attract a girl's attention. The design of the bottle is also important. There are even girls who collect perfumes solely for their containers.

Cosmetics

The focal point of every attractive young woman's makeup is her eyes. Girls with sparkling eyes are appealing: Everyone around them feels rejuvenated. On these pages are presented the most popular cosmetic items and a lesson in applying eye makeup. Naturally, there are many alternatives to applying makeup, and what is presented here is just one. Methods change with the times, and it pays to investigate the current makeup techniques.

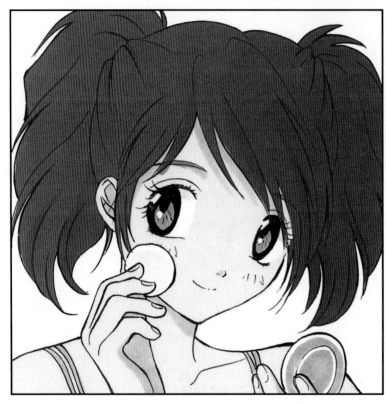

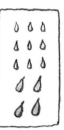

Teardrop-shaped bindi
A bindi was originally a vermilion dot worn on the forehead of a married Hindu woman. These bindi, shaped like teardrops, are designed to be worn anywhere on the body.

False eyelashes
False eyelashes are no longer the taboo items they once were, and perfectly normal young women can be seen wearing them. They come in various shades and even come trimmed and shaped.

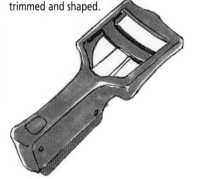

Eyelash curler
An eyelash curler works by placing the eyelashes between the crimpers and pressing.

Applying Eye Makeup

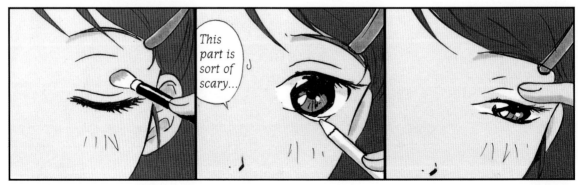

This part is sort of scary...

① First, using a sponge-tip applicator, apply a pastel eyeshadow to the upper lid from the inner corners to the areas just under the eyebrows.

② Next, apply eyeliner using an eye pencil. Add white eyeliner to the rim of the lower eyelid only.

③ Using that same white eye pencil, blend the eyeliner to the area from corner to corner of the eyes. Use the middle finger for better blending.

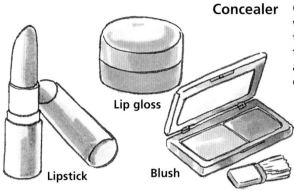

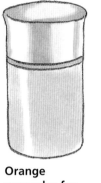

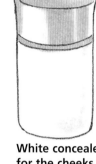

Lip gloss

Lipstick

Blush

Concealer

Concealer, the initial cosmetic applied to the skin, works wonders for controlling dark circles under the eyes or shiny, oily areas on the T-zone. After the concealer, the foundation is applied. Not applying concealer may result in over application of the foundation to compensate.

Lipstick, Lip Gloss and Blush

To achieve a natural look, apply lipstick from the center of the lip moving outward and blending. Add lip gloss over lipstick for a moist appearance. Blush is applied just below the cheekbone using a single sweep. Too much blush results in a garish appearance.

Orange concealer for underneath the eyes

White concealer for the cheeks and T-zone

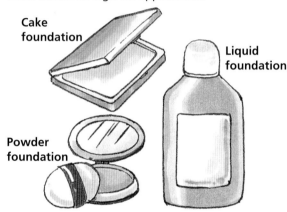

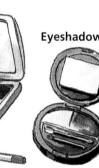

Cake foundation

Liquid foundation

Powder foundation

Mascara

Eyeshadow

Eyebrow color

Eye pencil

Foundations

Foundations come in various forms, including cake and liquid. Liquid foundations tend to be used more during the summer, owing to their light coverage. To finish, a powderpuff is used to blend the foundation thoroughly.

Eyebrow Color, Eyeshadow and Mascara

The eyebrows are first sculpted with a razor or eyebrow tweezers, and then the makeup is applied. The eyebrows require quite a bit of effort, since they must be cared for regularly. After the eyebrows are outlined with liner, the color is blended inward.

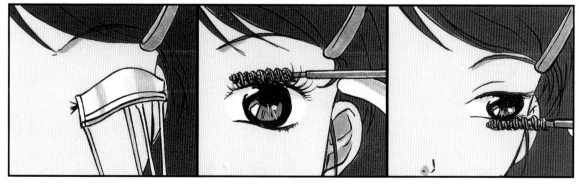

④ After the eyes come the eyelashes. First, the eyelashes are tightly crimped upward using an eyelash curler.

⑤ The pretty girl uses black mascara, which is brushed on thoroughly using upward strokes.

⑥ One mustn't forget the lower lashes. As with the upper lashes, the mascara is brushed in gentle strokes down along the lower lashes to give the effect give the effect of bright, wide-open eyes.

Lingerie Chest

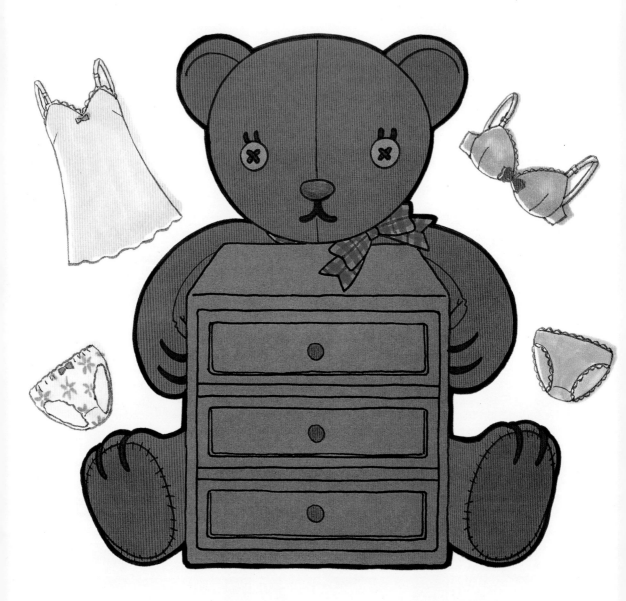

Girls often put perfumed soaps and sachets in their lingerie drawers to scent their undergarments. Women's undergarments cost considerably more than men's, so consequently, women put more effort into their undergarments' care. Each girl differs in the way she folds her intimate apparel. The next page shows a few such examples.

The Panties Drawer

Underpants are available in a variety of fabrics, from cotton to nylon to silk. Panties may come with lace frills, satin ribbons or elastic waistbands. Bikini-cut panties look attractive on young women, but as women grow older, the low cut may begin to emphasize bulges in the belly. Elastic waistbands vary in thickness, from no wider than a shoelace to up to an inch on sports briefs. Panties made of spandex become popular in the summer because they leave less marks on the body.

Pouch for packing panties on trips

Sachets are placed in the corners of the drawers.

The Brassier Drawer

The bustier, bras with removable straps, and seamless bras with smooth fronts are popular for the summer. Underwire bras ensure an attractive shape, but wireless bras are so much more comfortable. Women with smaller cup sizes often add inserts for extra volume.

Underwire bra

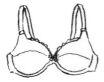

Seamless bra

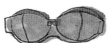

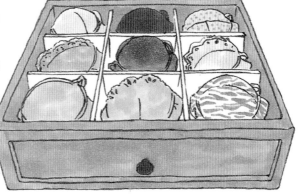

Bras are folded by matching up the cups and then tucking the straps inside.

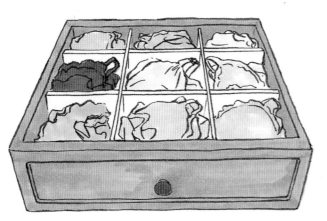

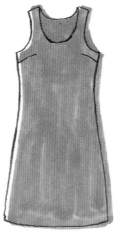

The Slip and Camisole Drawer

Slips and camisoles are primarily made of nylon. However, on that special night out, a girl enjoys the smooth feel of silk against her skin. Full slips are worn under sheer dresses with no lining.

Perfumed soaps and sachets are placed inside the larger compartments.

Bath Products

Girls love to take baths. A bathroom is much more than a place to wash. Bathing gives a girl the opportunity to scrutinize her body all over and lose herself in thought. It also provides some much needed time to stretch and loosen up those muscles. These reasons and more are why bath products carry so much value for young women.

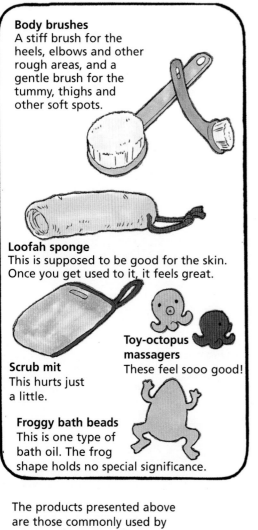

Body brushes
A stiff brush for the heels, elbows and other rough areas, and a gentle brush for the tummy, thighs and other soft spots.

Loofah sponge
This is supposed to be good for the skin. Once you get used to it, it feels great.

Toy-octopus massagers
These feel sooo good!

Scrub mit
This hurts just a little.

Froggy bath beads
This is one type of bath oil. The frog shape holds no special significance.

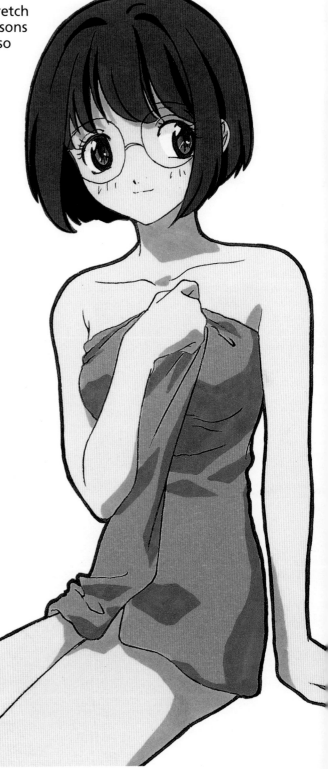

The products presented above are those commonly used by young women in Japan. So many delightful products appear on the store shelves today, it is difficult to know what to buy!

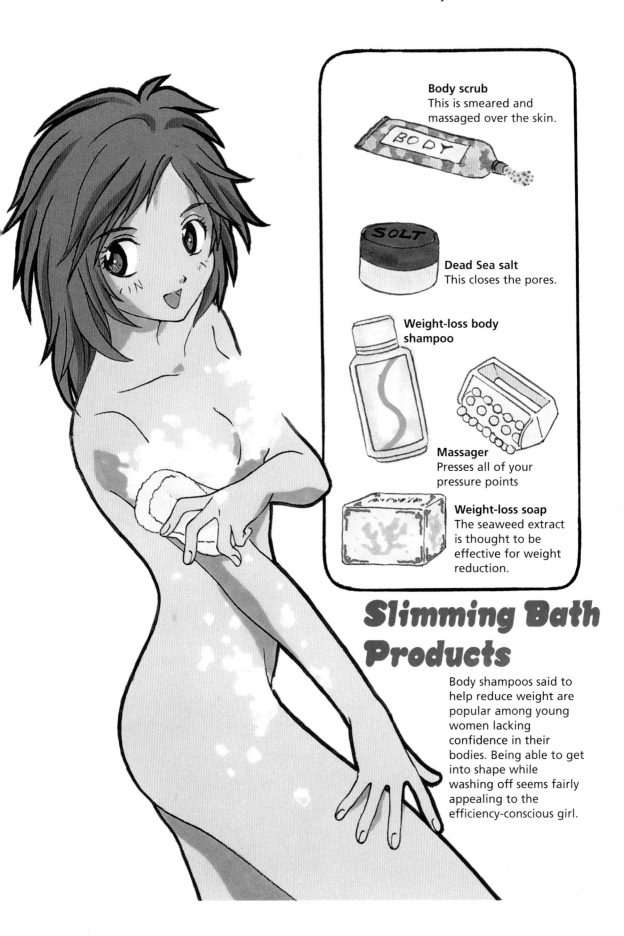

Body scrub
This is smeared and massaged over the skin.

Dead Sea salt
This closes the pores.

Weight-loss body shampoo

Massager
Presses all of your pressure points

Weight-loss soap
The seaweed extract is thought to be effective for weight reduction.

Slimming Bath Products

Body shampoos said to help reduce weight are popular among young women lacking confidence in their bodies. Being able to get into shape while washing off seems fairly appealing to the efficiency-conscious girl.

Removable Tattoos

Because these tattoos can be removed and changed with ease, they provide a fun opportunity for girls to experiment with a bold fashion statement. Tattoos can make one alluring or just plain cute, depending on where they are placed. Removable tattoos are not limited to decals: there are also professional artists who apply them using high-quality inks.

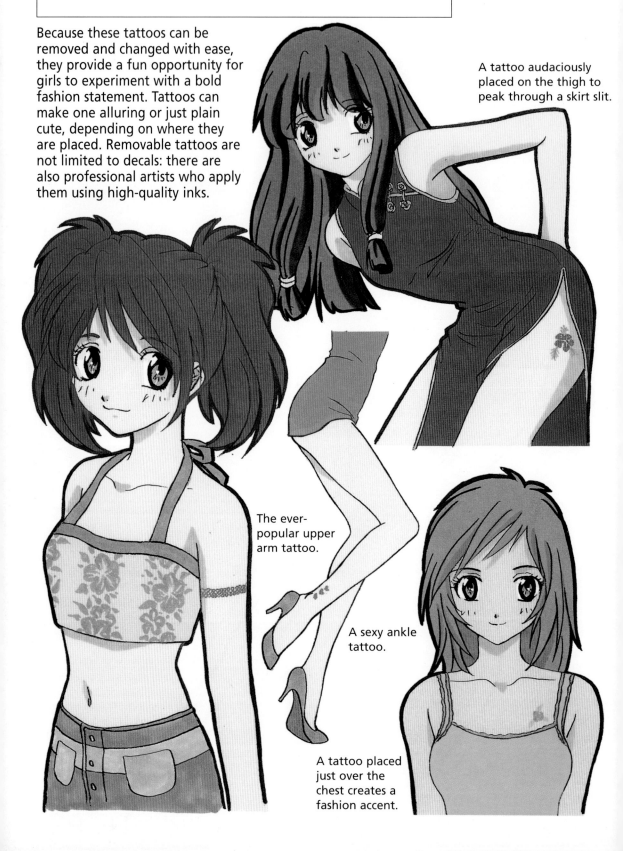

A tattoo audaciously placed on the thigh to peak through a skirt slit.

The ever-popular upper arm tattoo.

A sexy ankle tattoo.

A tattoo placed just over the chest creates a fashion accent.

Fashion Statements

Chapter 3

➡ Daywear

Girls do not always dress like the models in fashion magazines. On the next few pages appear some of the typical fashions preferred by young women.

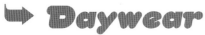

Perky Girl

To the right, I'm wearing a tight-fitting fleece top and a flared miniskirt. The top just barely covers my waist, which I think makes it look kind of cute. The arms have elasticized bands, making the shoulders all puffy. This outfit probably wouldn't be appropriate for someone who was timid about showing off her arms. On my legs, I am wearing thigh-high socks, and on my feet, a pair of Mary Janes. The Mary Janes are suede on the outside, which makes them an unusual design.

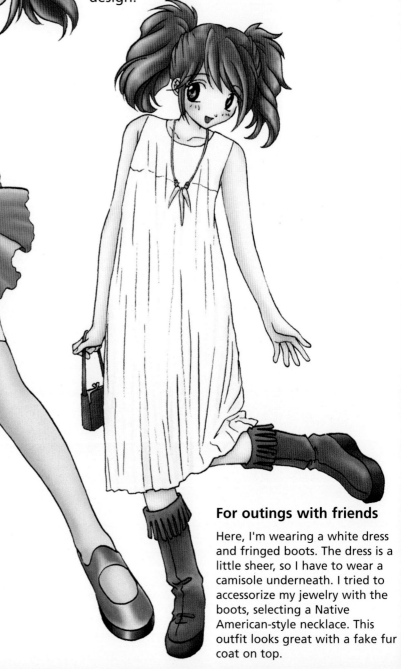

For outings with friends

Here, I'm wearing a white dress and fringed boots. The dress is a little sheer, so I have to wear a camisole underneath. I tried to accessorize my jewelry with the boots, selecting a Native American-style necklace. This outfit looks great with a fake fur coat on top.

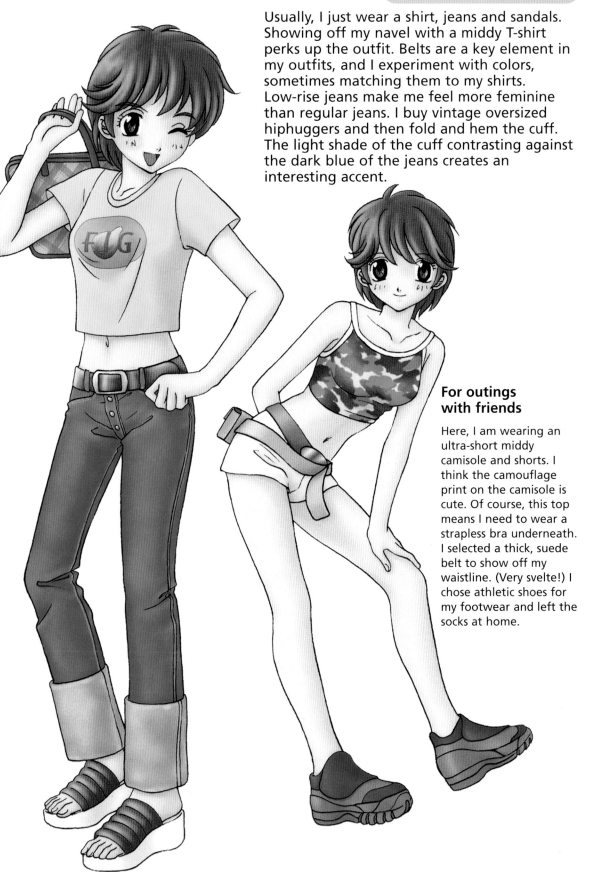

Sporty Girl

Usually, I just wear a shirt, jeans and sandals. Showing off my navel with a middy T-shirt perks up the outfit. Belts are a key element in my outfits, and I experiment with colors, sometimes matching them to my shirts. Low-rise jeans make me feel more feminine than regular jeans. I buy vintage oversized hiphuggers and then fold and hem the cuff. The light shade of the cuff contrasting against the dark blue of the jeans creates an interesting accent.

For outings with friends

Here, I am wearing an ultra-short middy camisole and shorts. I think the camouflage print on the camisole is cute. Of course, this top means I need to wear a strapless bra underneath. I selected a thick, suede belt to show off my waistline. (Very svelte!) I chose athletic shoes for my footwear and left the socks at home.

Dreamy Girl

I strive for an ultra-feminine look. The bias on this tunic tucks under the bust, and then the rest of the tunic billows out. The armholes are wide, so the back needed some alteration. Since the tunic reached down to my bottom, I adjusted the shoulder seam a bit. Now the hemline falls just below the hips, preventing my legs from looking too short, which makes me happy.

I matched the tunic with flared Capri pants to give the entire outfit a feminine feel.
The best length for capris like this is mid-calf. Silver platform crossover sandals create a soft finish.

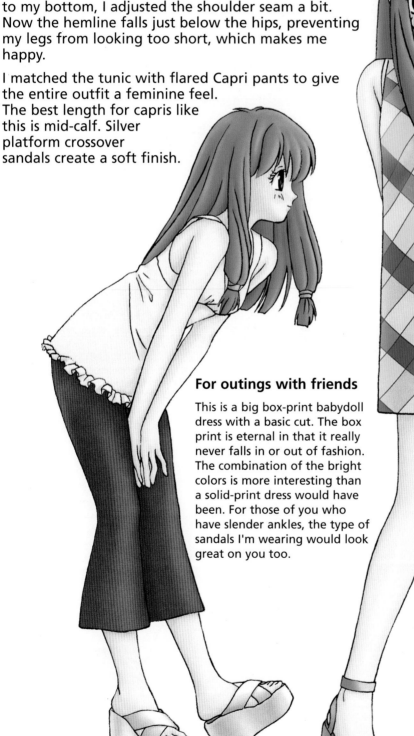

For outings with friends

This is a big box-print babydoll dress with a basic cut. The box print is eternal in that it really never falls in or out of fashion. The combination of the bright colors is more interesting than a solid-print dress would have been. For those of you who have slender ankles, the type of sandals I'm wearing would look great on you too.

Precocious Girl

The sleeveless top I'm wearing has a Nehru collar and is done in basic colors. The clean cut of the collar generates a tailored look. Vertical stripes are said to be slimming. The lower half consists of a skirt and slacks. The doubling of the two sort of gives the outfit an ethnic feel. The colors are pretty muted overall, so this bright red bag really ties the outfit together. The red sandals match the handbag.

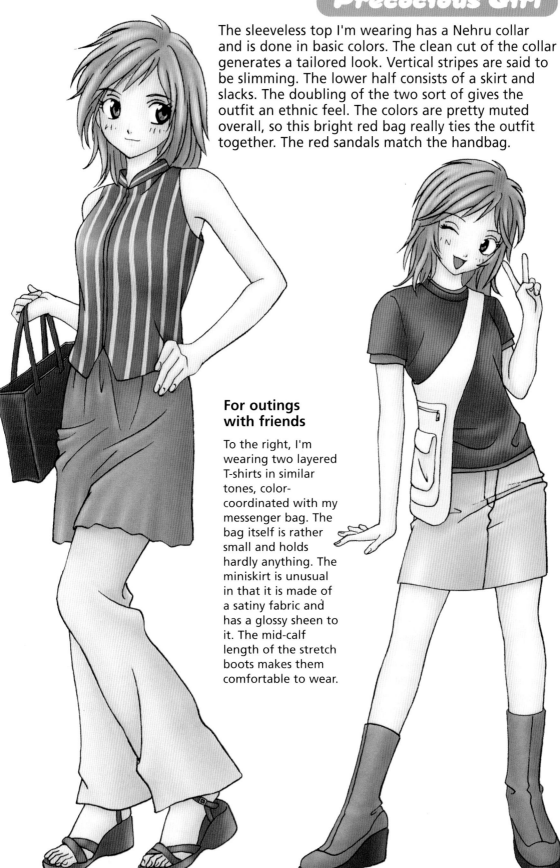

For outings with friends

To the right, I'm wearing two layered T-shirts in similar tones, color-coordinated with my messenger bag. The bag itself is rather small and holds hardly anything. The miniskirt is unusual in that it is made of a satiny fabric and has a glossy sheen to it. The mid-calf length of the stretch boots makes them comfortable to wear.

Shy Girl

I'm wearing a camisole and flared skirt with an ethnic-design border. A camisole with some width to its straps provides a softer look. This design is for girls who like to show off their collarbones. I pulled the ribbon tight to get the bodice to ruffle. I find the ethnic-toned, robin's-egg blue refreshing, but trying to prevent the color from fading when I wash it is a nuisance. My sandals aren't fussy: I just slip my bare feet into them.

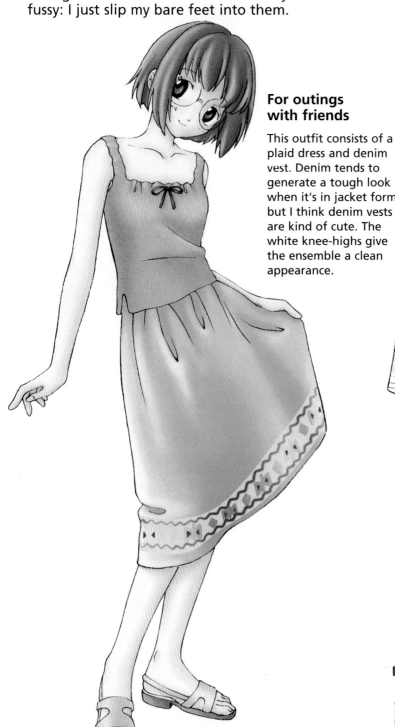

For outings with friends

This outfit consists of a plaid dress and denim vest. Denim tends to generate a tough look when it's in jacket form, but I think denim vests are kind of cute. The white knee-highs give the ensemble a clean appearance.

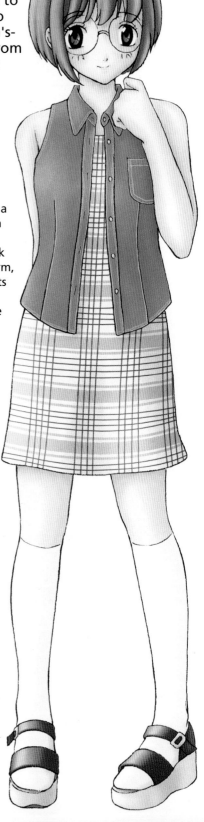

Uppity Girl

You might be surprised to learn that the lonesome girl wraps herself in fashion for protection. I tend to wear vivid colors and boldly cut designs. I zealously incorporate trendy items into even in my everyday dress. Here, I am wearing an arm warmer and sleeveless sweater set. The wraparound skirt was designed to have a mismatched hemline. The fitted suede boots generate a trim appearance.

For outings with friends

Here I am wearing a winter wool suit with a detachable fur collar and matching fur skirt hem. Patent leather heels make this outfit perfect for parties.

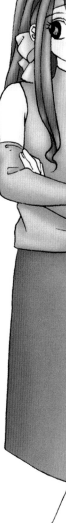

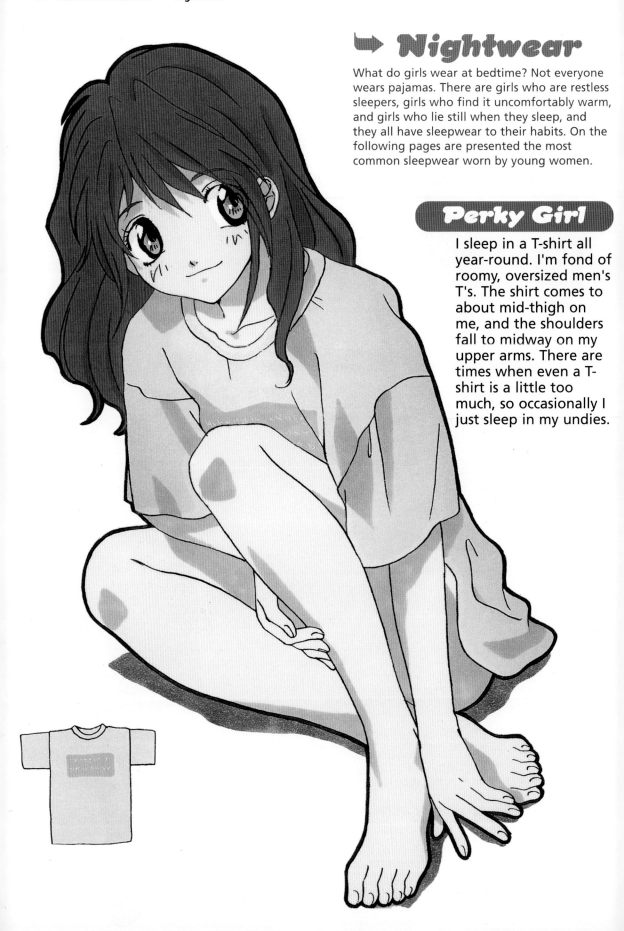

➧ Nightwear

What do girls wear at bedtime? Not everyone wears pajamas. There are girls who are restless sleepers, girls who find it uncomfortably warm, and girls who lie still when they sleep, and they all have sleepwear to their habits. On the following pages are presented the most common sleepwear worn by young women.

Perky Girl

I sleep in a T-shirt all year-round. I'm fond of roomy, oversized men's T's. The shirt comes to about mid-thigh on me, and the shoulders fall to midway on my upper arms. There are times when even a T-shirt is a little too much, so occasionally I just sleep in my undies.

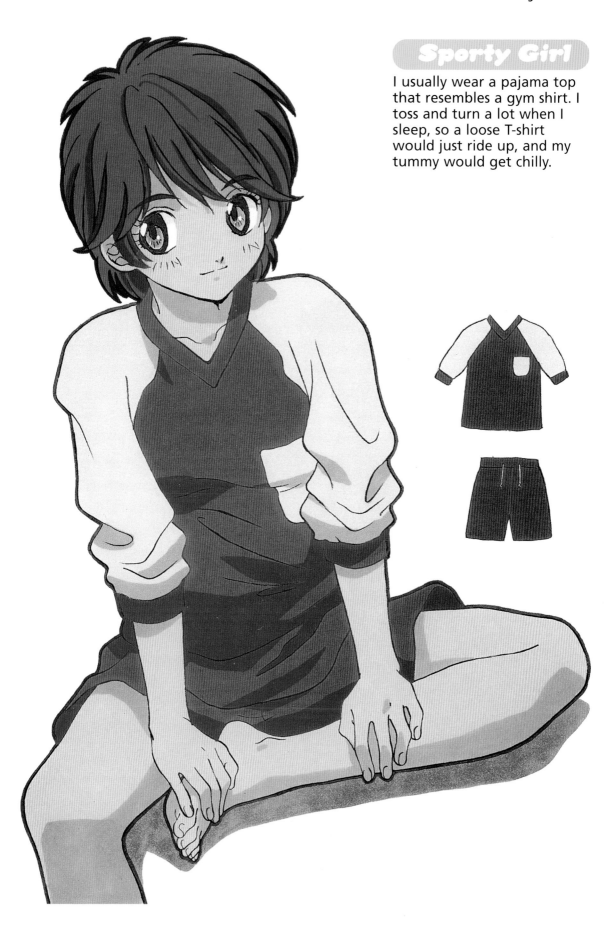

Sporty Girl

I usually wear a pajama top that resembles a gym shirt. I toss and turn a lot when I sleep, so a loose T-shirt would just ride up, and my tummy would get chilly.

Dreamy Girl

I have a teddy bear-print nightgown that's my favorite. I just love soft and roomy cotton nightgowns. I also wear floral-print nighties or nighties with oodles of lace ruffles. As you might expect, I sleep with my teddy.

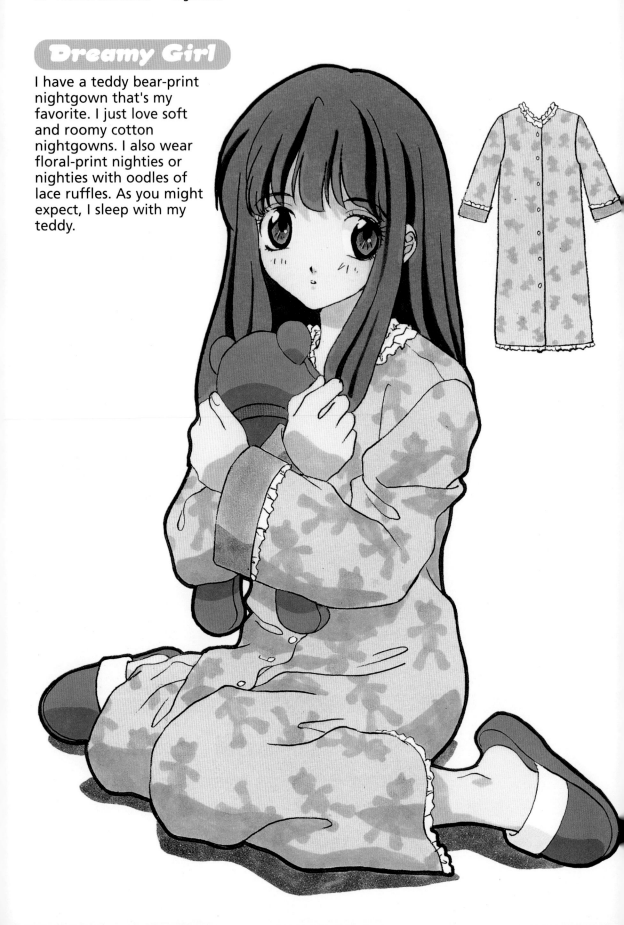

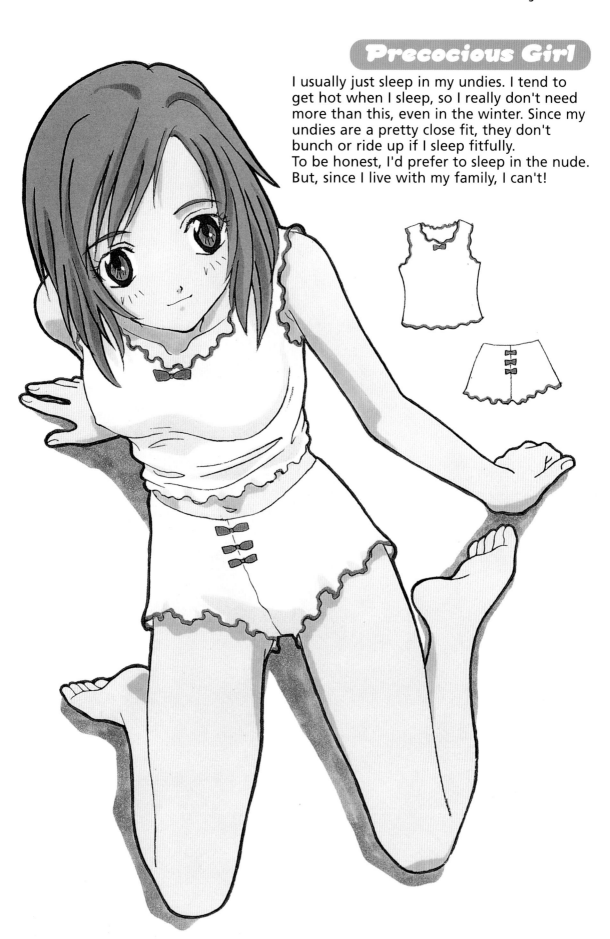

Precocious Girl

I usually just sleep in my undies. I tend to get hot when I sleep, so I really don't need more than this, even in the winter. Since my undies are a pretty close fit, they don't bunch or ride up if I sleep fitfully.
To be honest, I'd prefer to sleep in the nude. But, since I live with my family, I can't!

Shy Girl

I embarrass easily, so I don't like to expose myself when I sleep. My favorite things to wear are flannel pajamas with floral prints, particularly tulips. I like the nightgowns that are sold for girls, but I am a surprisingly fitful sleeper, so pajamas are enough to keep me comfy.

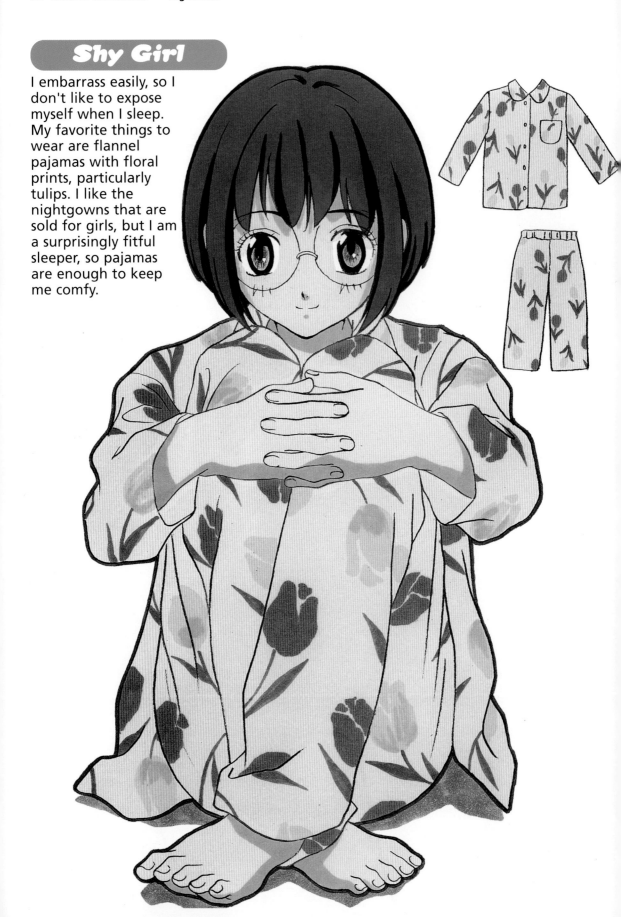

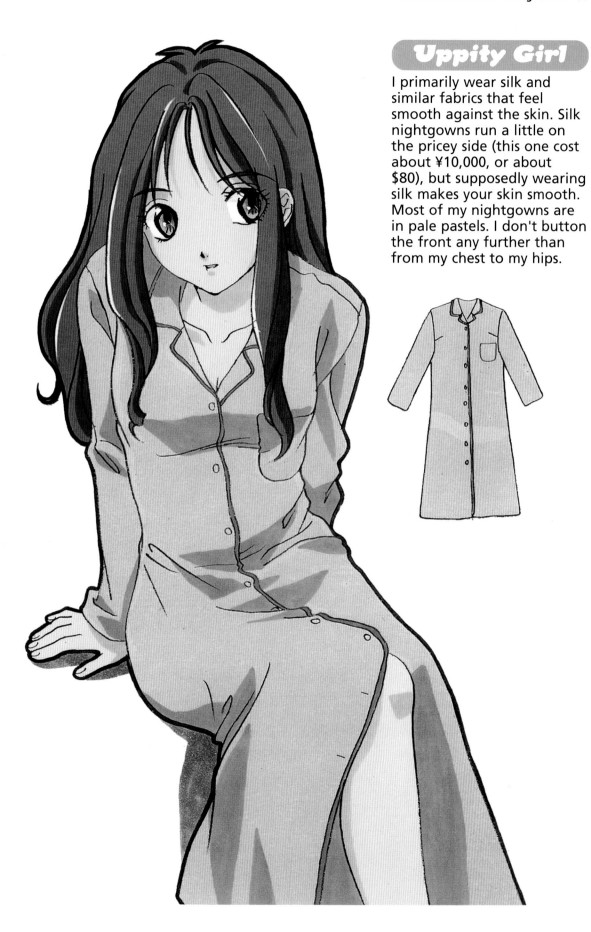

Uppity Girl

I primarily wear silk and similar fabrics that feel smooth against the skin. Silk nightgowns run a little on the pricey side (this one cost about ¥10,000, or about $80), but supposedly wearing silk makes your skin smooth. Most of my nightgowns are in pale pastels. I don't button the front any further than from my chest to my hips.

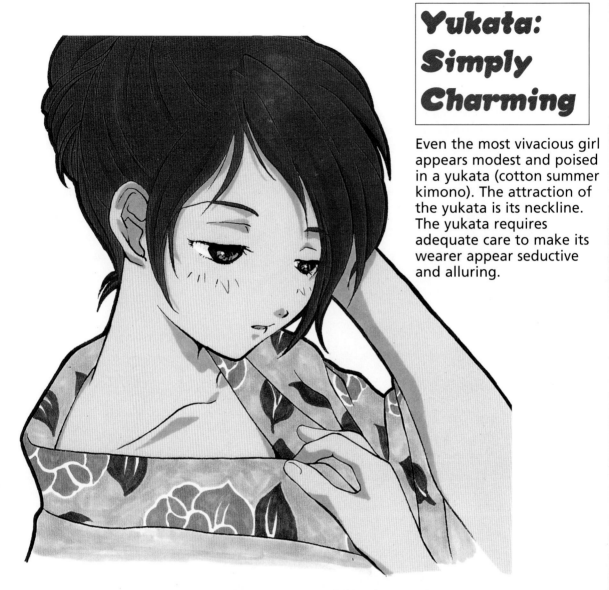

Yukata: Simply Charming

Even the most vivacious girl appears modest and poised in a yukata (cotton summer kimono). The attraction of the yukata is its neckline. The yukata requires adequate care to make its wearer appear seductive and alluring.

Girls dressed in kimono on New Year's Day or at festivals always appear striking. However, in terms of price, comfort and ease of care (the kimono requires dry cleaning), the yukata is by far the costume of choice. Yet, despite their culture, Japanese girls today sadly find it difficult to coordinate a yukata as easily as they do Western clothing.

Tying the Obi (sash)   This looks difficult at first glance, but it is surprisingly easy.

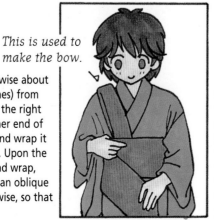

This is used to make the bow.

① Fold the obi lengthwise about 50 centimeters (20 inches) from the end, and rest it on the right shoulder. Bring the other end of the obi around front and wrap it around the waist once. Upon the beginning of the second wrap, bring the obi down at an oblique angle and fold lengthwise, so that the fold faces up.

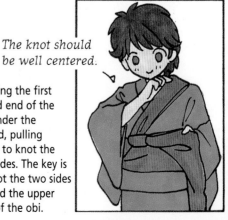

The knot should be well centered.

② Bring the first folded end of the obi under the second, pulling firmly to knot the two sides. The key is to knot the two sides toward the upper part of the obi.

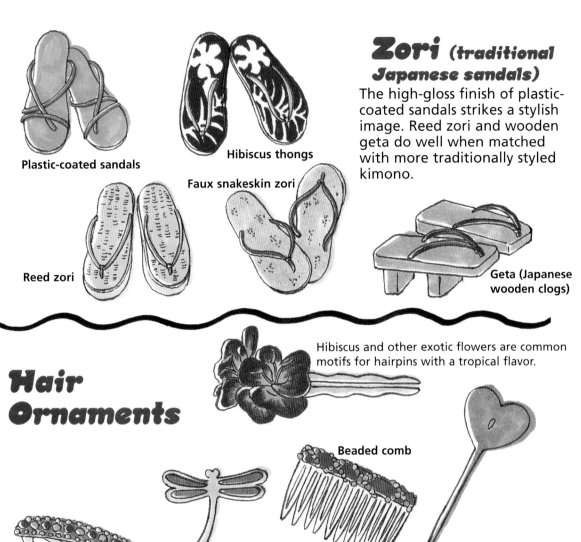

Plastic-coated sandals

Hibiscus thongs

Faux snakeskin zori

Reed zori

Zori (traditional Japanese sandals)

The high-gloss finish of plastic-coated sandals strikes a stylish image. Reed zori and wooden geta do well when matched with more traditionally styled kimono.

Geta (Japanese wooden clogs)

Hair Ornaments

Hibiscus and other exotic flowers are common motifs for hairpins with a tropical flavor.

Beaded comb

Dragonfly-shaped hairpin

Heart-shaped wooden hairpin

Glittering rhinestone barrette

③ Next comes the bow. (This is ultimately slid to the back.) Take a 40-centimeter (15-inch) segment from the straggling end of the obi and fold it back. Repeat over and over, folding each 40-centimeter segment accordion-style. Once the end is totally folded, draw in the center to form a butterfly shape, creating a hill and two valleys in the middle. Hold this firmly.

This end gets wrapped around the bow.

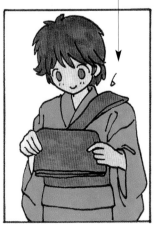

④ Bring the other end of the obi resting on the shoulder down and once around the center of the butterfly bow. Tuck the loose end into the obi, while adjusting and balancing the right and left side of the bow.

This part is tucked inside the obi.

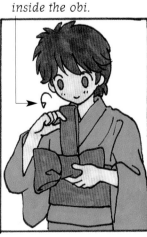

Slide the bow to the back, and you're done!

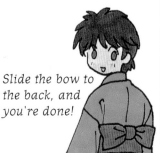

➥ Various Yukata

The design of the yukata is selected based on one's body type or facial features. Recently, bold new designs have been making a prominent appearance in stores. Even if a girl's facial features are a little more prominent than a classic Japanese face, there are still many complementary styles available.

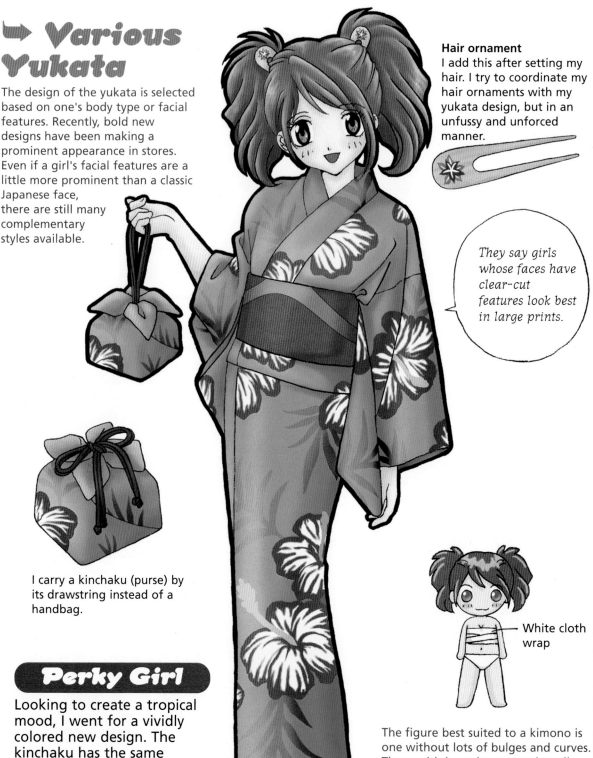

Hair ornament
I add this after setting my hair. I try to coordinate my hair ornaments with my yukata design, but in an unfussy and unforced manner.

They say girls whose faces have clear-cut features look best in large prints.

I carry a kinchaku (purse) by its drawstring instead of a handbag.

Perky Girl

Looking to create a tropical mood, I went for a vividly colored new design. The kinchaku has the same pattern, resulting in a colorful ensemble overall. In contrast, clean and simple black zori look best with a design like this.

← White cloth wrap

The figure best suited to a kimono is one without lots of bulges and curves. Those with large breasts and small hips (or vice versa) should flatten their chests using a cloth wrap or widen their waists using a towel. The key is to eliminate curves as much as possible.

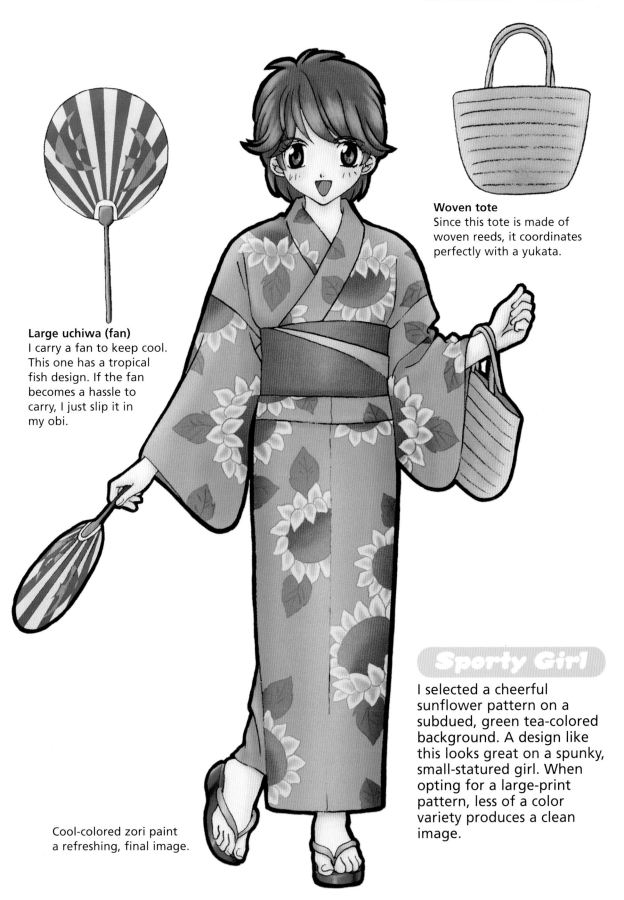

Woven tote
Since this tote is made of woven reeds, it coordinates perfectly with a yukata.

Large uchiwa (fan)
I carry a fan to keep cool. This one has a tropical fish design. If the fan becomes a hassle to carry, I just slip it in my obi.

Sporty Girl

I selected a cheerful sunflower pattern on a subdued, green tea-colored background. A design like this looks great on a spunky, small-statured girl. When opting for a large-print pattern, less of a color variety produces a clean image.

Cool-colored zori paint a refreshing, final image.

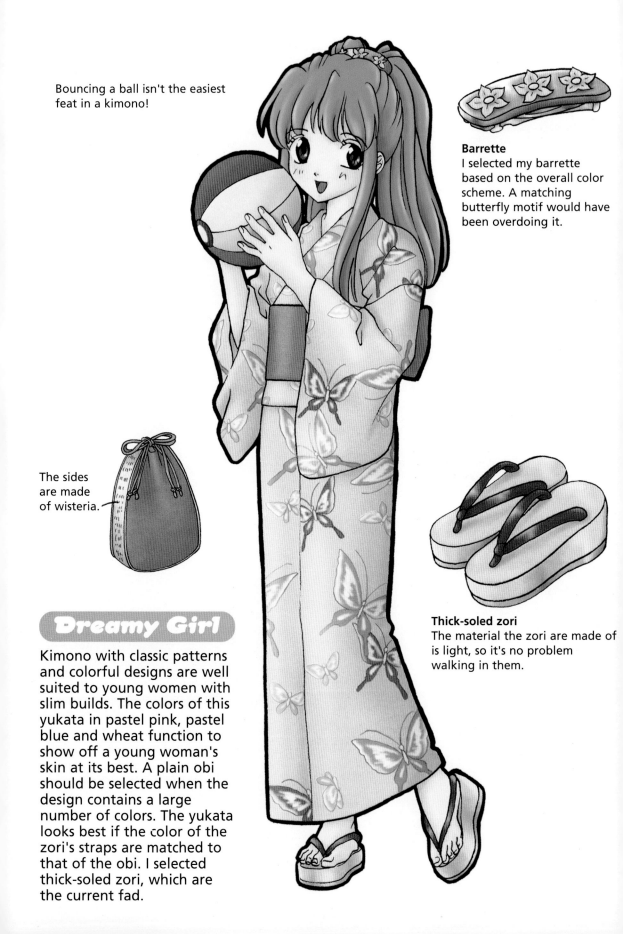

Bouncing a ball isn't the easiest feat in a kimono!

Barrette
I selected my barrette based on the overall color scheme. A matching butterfly motif would have been overdoing it.

The sides are made of wisteria.

Thick-soled zori
The material the zori are made of is light, so it's no problem walking in them.

Dreamy Girl

Kimono with classic patterns and colorful designs are well suited to young women with slim builds. The colors of this yukata in pastel pink, pastel blue and wheat function to show off a young woman's skin at its best. A plain obi should be selected when the design contains a large number of colors. The yukata looks best if the color of the zori's straps are matched to that of the obi. I selected thick-soled zori, which are the current fad.

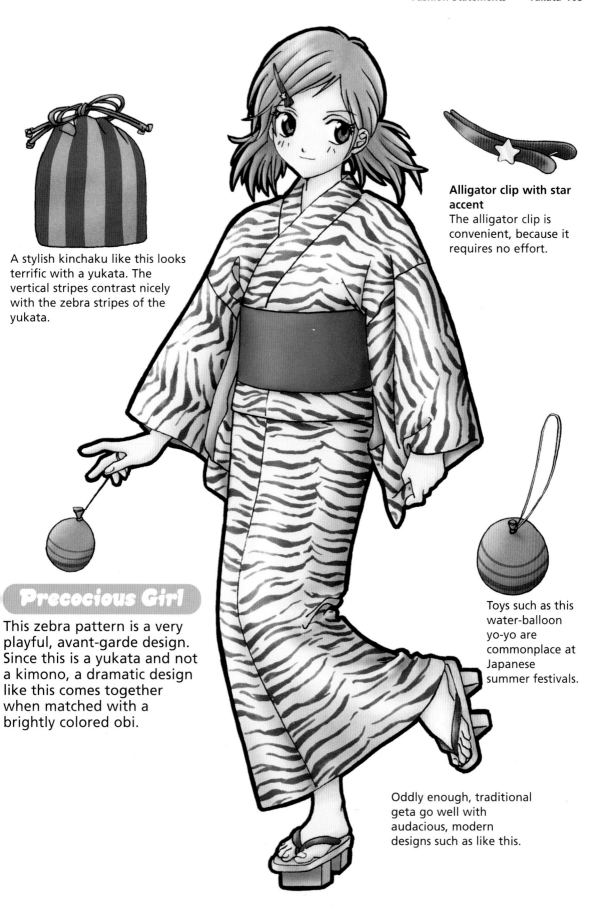

A stylish kinchaku like this looks terrific with a yukata. The vertical stripes contrast nicely with the zebra stripes of the yukata.

Alligator clip with star accent
The alligator clip is convenient, because it requires no effort.

Precocious Girl

This zebra pattern is a very playful, avant-garde design. Since this is a yukata and not a kimono, a dramatic design like this comes together when matched with a brightly colored obi.

Toys such as this water-balloon yo-yo are commonplace at Japanese summer festivals.

Oddly enough, traditional geta go well with audacious, modern designs such as like this.

Even a girl with short hair can have fun with mini-hair clips such as these.

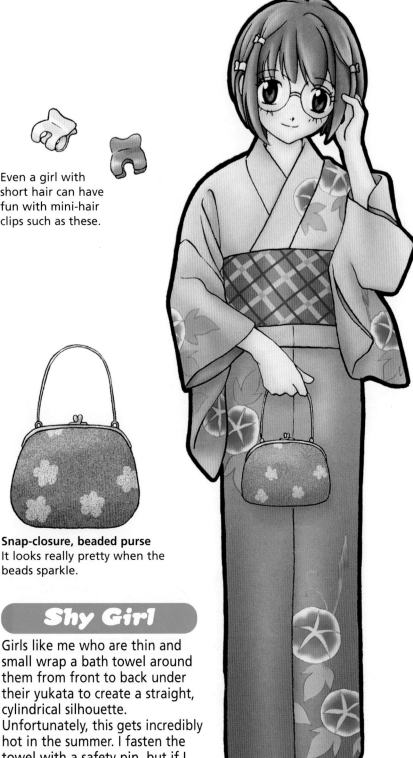

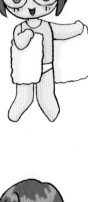

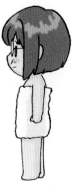

Snap-closure, beaded purse
It looks really pretty when the beads sparkle.

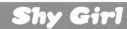

Shy Girl

Girls like me who are thin and small wrap a bath towel around them from front to back under their yukata to create a straight, cylindrical silhouette. Unfortunately, this gets incredibly hot in the summer. I fasten the towel with a safety pin, but if I forget to wrap my obi tightly enough, then the towel shifts and comes loose. Even a classic yukata such as this one can take on a cute appearance with the right obi.

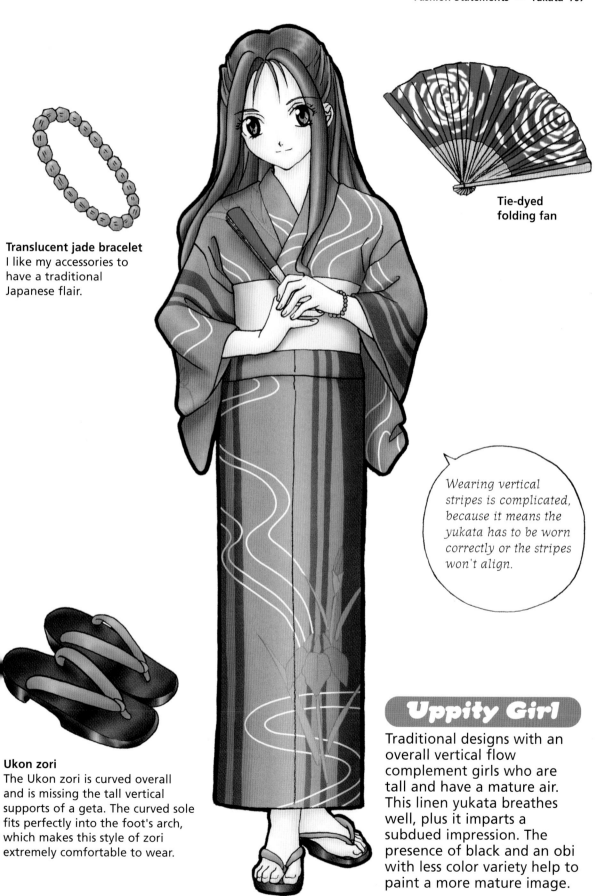

Tie-dyed folding fan

Translucent jade bracelet
I like my accessories to have a traditional Japanese flair.

Wearing vertical stripes is complicated, because it means the yukata has to be worn correctly or the stripes won't align.

Ukon zori
The Ukon zori is curved overall and is missing the tall vertical supports of a geta. The curved sole fits perfectly into the foot's arch, which makes this style of zori extremely comfortable to wear.

Uppity Girl

Traditional designs with an overall vertical flow complement girls who are tall and have a mature air. This linen yukata breathes well, plus it imparts a subdued impression. The presence of black and an obi with less color variety help to paint a more mature image.

Lingerie

Teddy
This is a one-piece garment similar in design to a swimsuit.

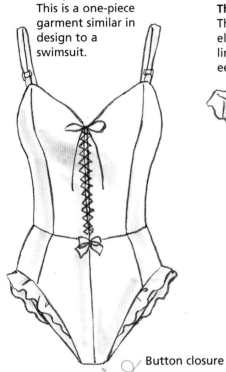

Button closure

Thong
This undergarment eliminates unsightly lines by using just an eensy bit of cloth.

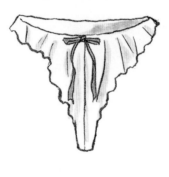

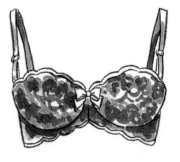

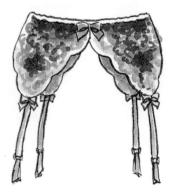

Brassiere and garter belt

Back view

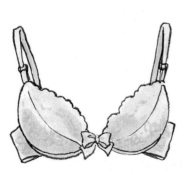

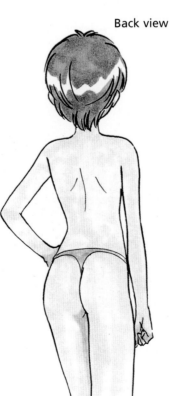

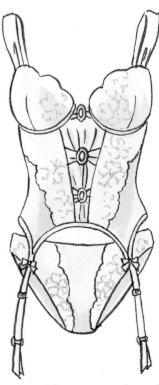

Bustier with garters and panties

Lace brassiere and panties
Both pieces are made almost entirely of lace.

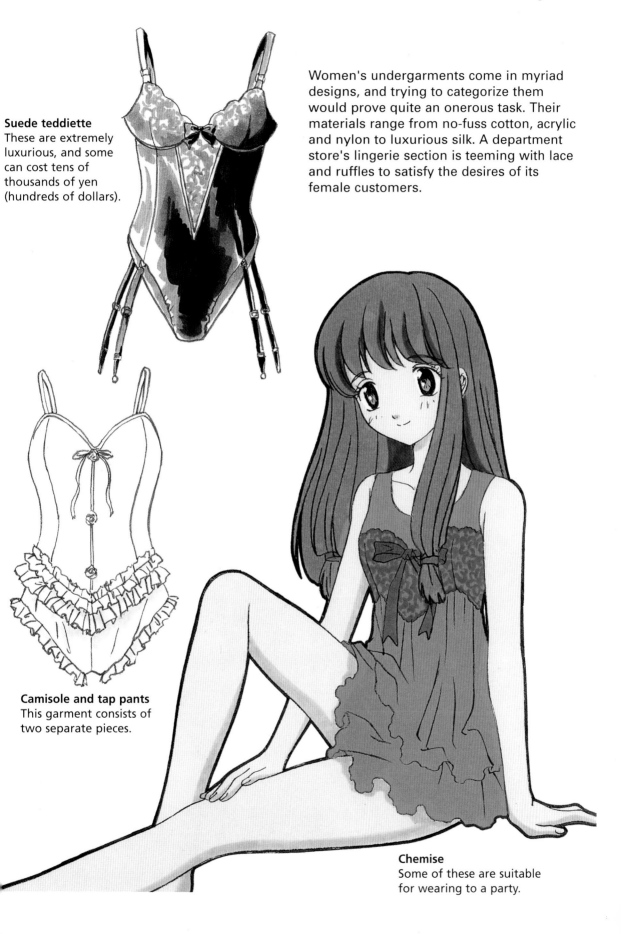

Suede teddiette
These are extremely luxurious, and some can cost tens of thousands of yen (hundreds of dollars).

Women's undergarments come in myriad designs, and trying to categorize them would prove quite an onerous task. Their materials range from no-fuss cotton, acrylic and nylon to luxurious silk. A department store's lingerie section is teeming with lace and ruffles to satisfy the desires of its female customers.

Camisole and tap pants
This garment consists of two separate pieces.

Chemise
Some of these are suitable for wearing to a party.

On the following pages is a categorization of undergarments according to the personality of their wearers. Rather than thinking of their body types, these girls seem to select their intimate apparel based solely on what they like.

Perky Girl

My undies tend to be cotton and with minimal lace—purely comfortable stuff. I go for charming touches like tiny bows and floral patterns.

I wear lined, underwire bras. These provide pushup shaping, so they look good even on girls of larger sizes.

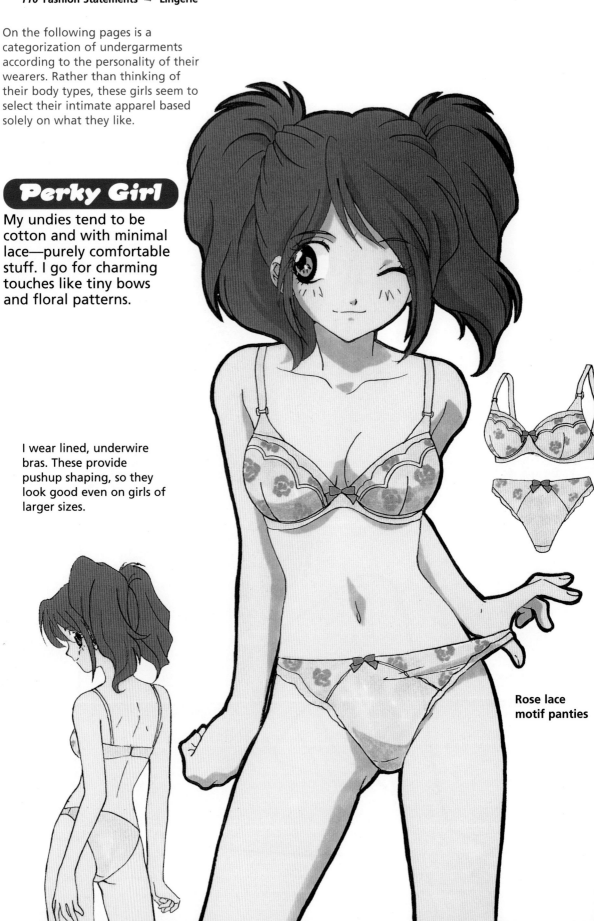

Rose lace motif panties

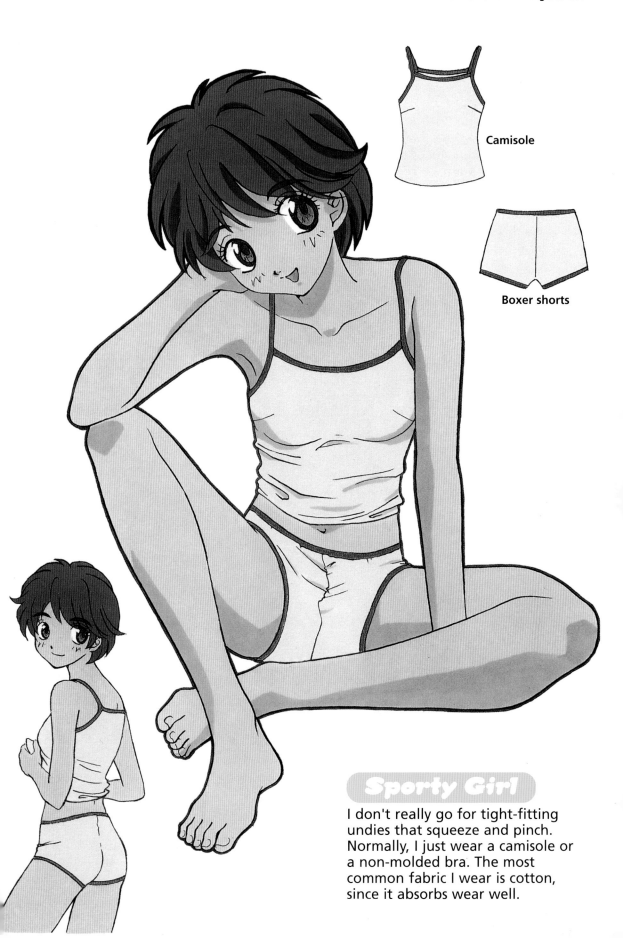

Camisole

Boxer shorts

Sporty Girl

I don't really go for tight-fitting undies that squeeze and pinch. Normally, I just wear a camisole or a non-molded bra. The most common fabric I wear is cotton, since it absorbs wear well.

Dreamy Girl

At first glance, this appears to be a glamorous chemise, but the tiny satin bows where the shoulder straps and front of the chemise are tied indicate my penchant for a "cute" look. These bows aren't fixed. I can play around, changing the color of the straps to match my mood. The color is a very girlish cherry pink.

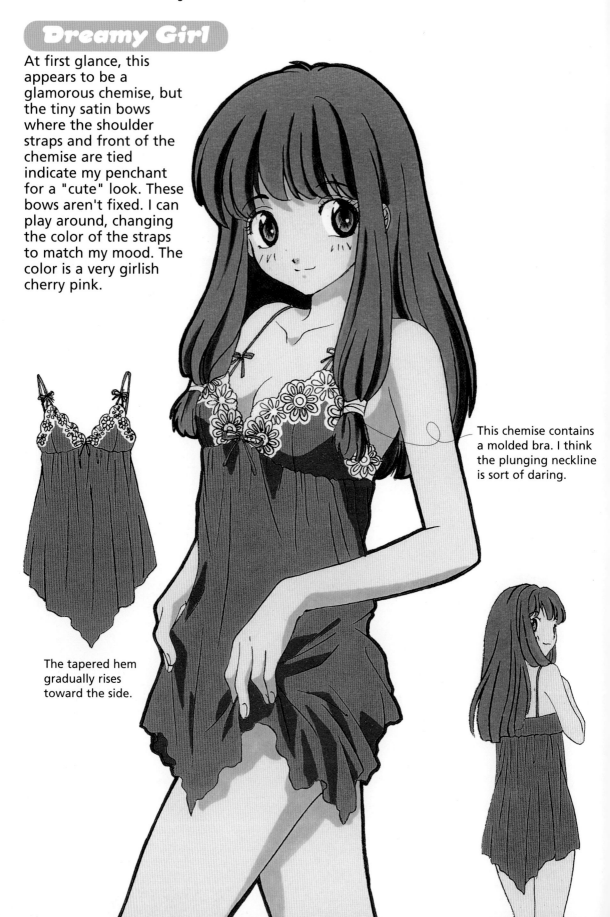

This chemise contains a molded bra. I think the plunging neckline is sort of daring.

The tapered hem gradually rises toward the side.

Precocious Girl

You'd be surprised at the number of girls who at first glance seem conservative about their undergarments, yet actually own extremely sexy unmentionables. Here, I am wearing a very audacious bustier, garter belt and panties set. As you probably surmised, this is not something I would wear to school. Still, I really enjoy secretly dressing like this and admiring myself in the mirror.

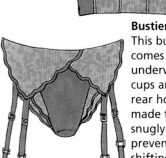

Bustier
This bustier comes with underwire cups and a rear hook. It is made to fit snugly and prevent shifting.

Garter belt and panties
The panties are of a very daring design. I wonder if leaving off the garter belts would reveal too much skin?

The length of the garter is adjusted here.

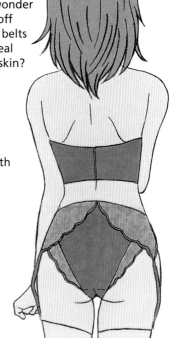

Shy Girl

I'm a homespun kind of girl and prefer undergarments that are comfy; appearance is secondary. This green-striped bra-and-panies set is made of cotton and feels great against my skin. They have just the teensiest bit of lace, which I think is pretty. The overall look is crisp and clean, which makes this set perfect for school.

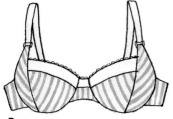

Bra
The cups are full, providing total coverage.

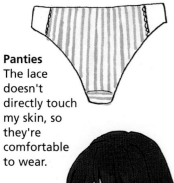

Panties
The lace doesn't directly touch my skin, so they're comfortable to wear.

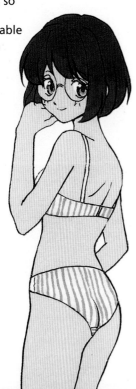

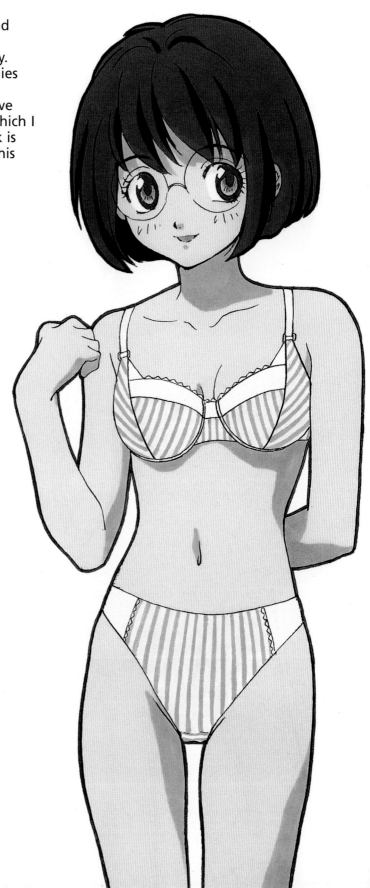

Uppity Posh

Girls who like to make themselves appear mature have a penchant for lingerie. I myself prefer fabrics with a sheen, such as satin and silk, and am inclined to purchase the more expensive garments. I usually lounge in my underwear, wearing a robe on top. I am fond of wireless bras, which are more comfortable. Most of my undergarments are lacy and can't be put in the washing machine.

Non-lined brassiere
Bras like these require confidence in one's body.

Panties
These panties come with a wide elastic band, so they don't pinch. The lace is made of a soft fabric, so it doesn't feel rough against my skin.

Bathrobes and Bath Wraps

The first thing a girl does when she hops out of the tub is wrap herself her in an oversized towel. But luxuriating in a stylish robe is every young woman's fantasy.

Incidentally, something called a "bath wrap," which is really nothing more than a bath towel with some sort of fastener, is very popular in the United States. The one modeled below is a simple design with a Velcro closure. Given the attractiveness, the comfort and the ease of care of these garments, they are quickly rising in popularity in Japan as well.

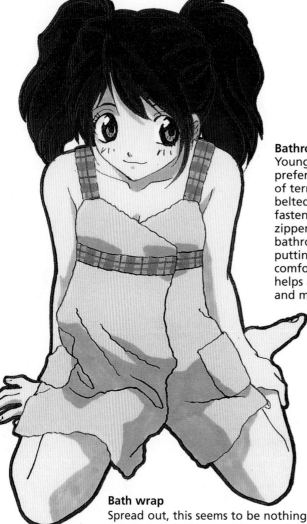

Bathrobe
Young women tend to prefer bathrobes made of terrycloth that are belted rather than fastened with buttons or zippers. Wearing a bathrobe a bit before putting on underwear is comfortable in that it helps absorb perspiration and makes skin smooth.

Bath wrap
Spread out, this seems to be nothing more than a bath towel. This one is fastened with Velcro, which makes it easy to slip on and let your skin cool of after taking a hot bath.

The Bare Essentials

Chapter 4

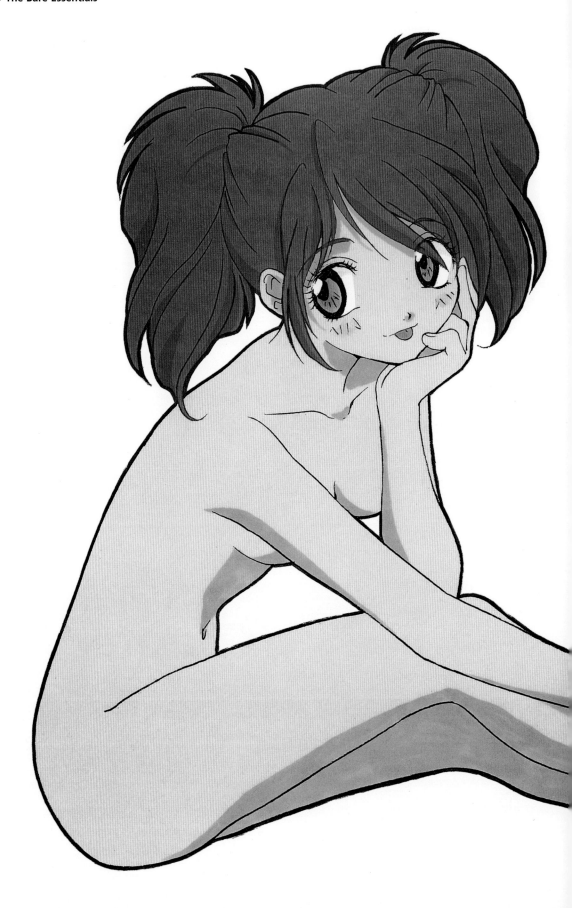

Illustrations of girls in the nude do not necessarily have to reveal all of their charms. The concept behind this section is to show artists how they can draw alluring images of their characters without exposing much more than perhaps the derriere. On the following pages are few poses that effectively illustrate how strategically concealing the private parts can actually be very erotic.

Perky Girl

This is a nude shot of my full figure. My skin is smooth, and I am completely confident with my body. I don't suffer from any feelings of inferiority. Well...that shot of my backside is a bit embarrassing...

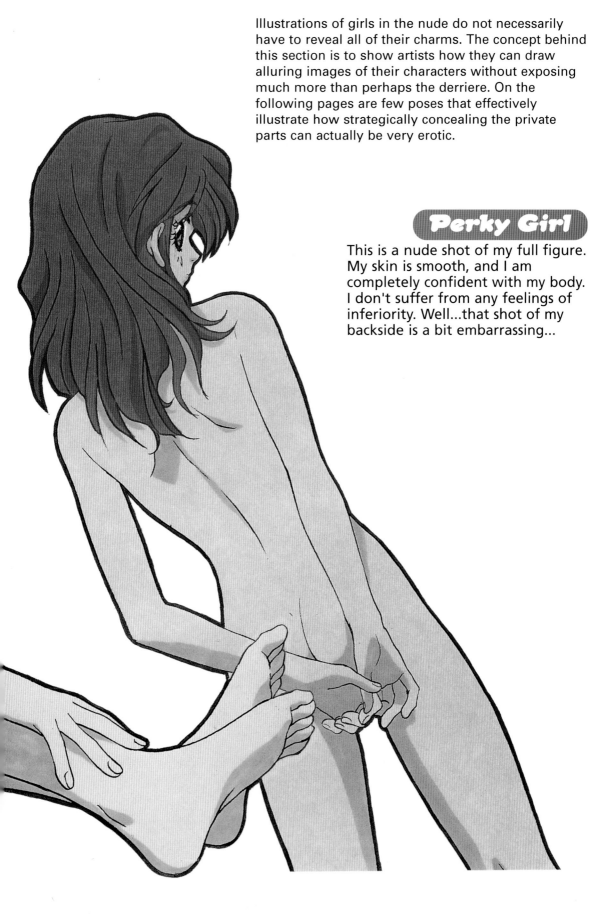

Sporty Girl

So, do you think a realistic shot like this is a bit too risqué? I'm a pretty candid person, so I have absolutely no problem with this pose. I'm actually having fun posing in the nude and am totally unembarassed. On the contrary, I think this is healthy. Oh yeah. Edit out the "details," OK? Don't go overboard trying to show every bit of a girl. Pretend you can't see these "details."

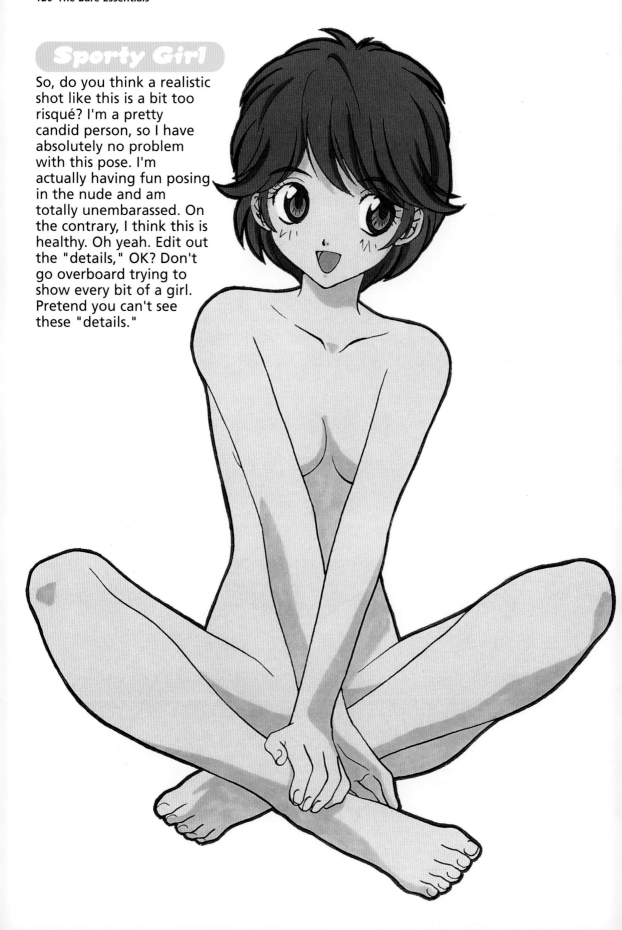

Dreamy Girl

A truly classical nude pose is to use her hair to hide your character's breasts. Maybe this pose is a last resort once you've exhausted showing her from the back or using her hands to cover her breasts! Well, whatever the case, this is a pose you can only use with characters that have long hair (like me), so it kind of puts you in a spot. Avoid a fully frontal view, OK?

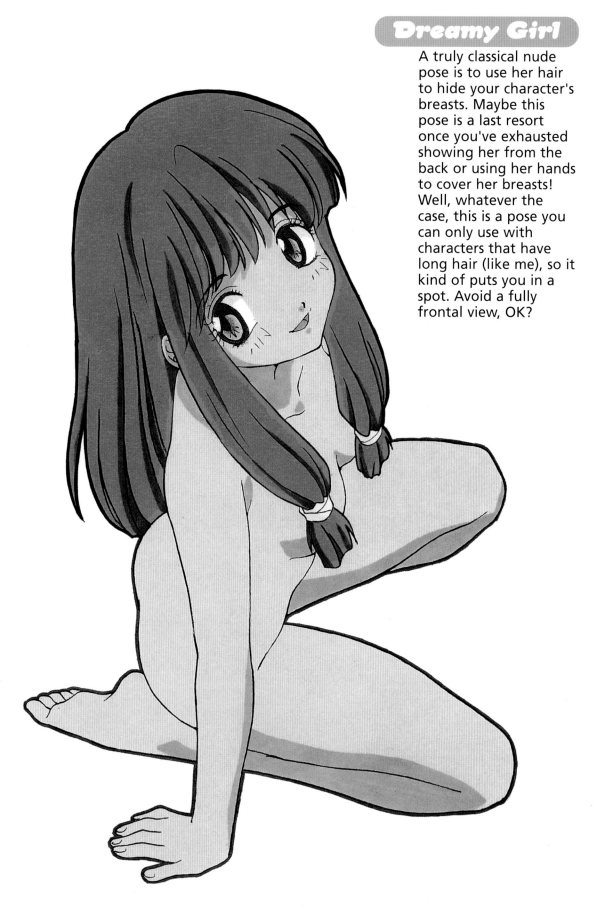

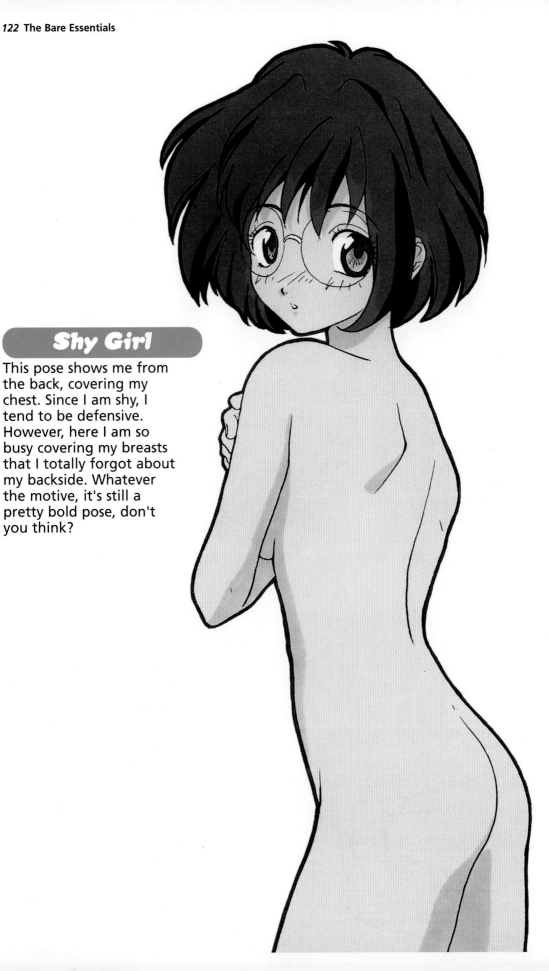

Shy Girl

This pose shows me from the back, covering my chest. Since I am shy, I tend to be defensive. However, here I am so busy covering my breasts that I totally forgot about my backside. Whatever the motive, it's still a pretty bold pose, don't you think?

Precocious Girl

I may come across as assertive, but I'm actually pretty shy. Here I sit, covering my breasts—a rather conservative pose. I was drawn with my head tilted forward ever so slightly to convey my embarrassment. If my feet were to shift just a few inches either way, everything would be exposed, so take care when you draw your own character. If she seems in trouble, rotate her lower body just a little to hide what she doesn't want others to see.

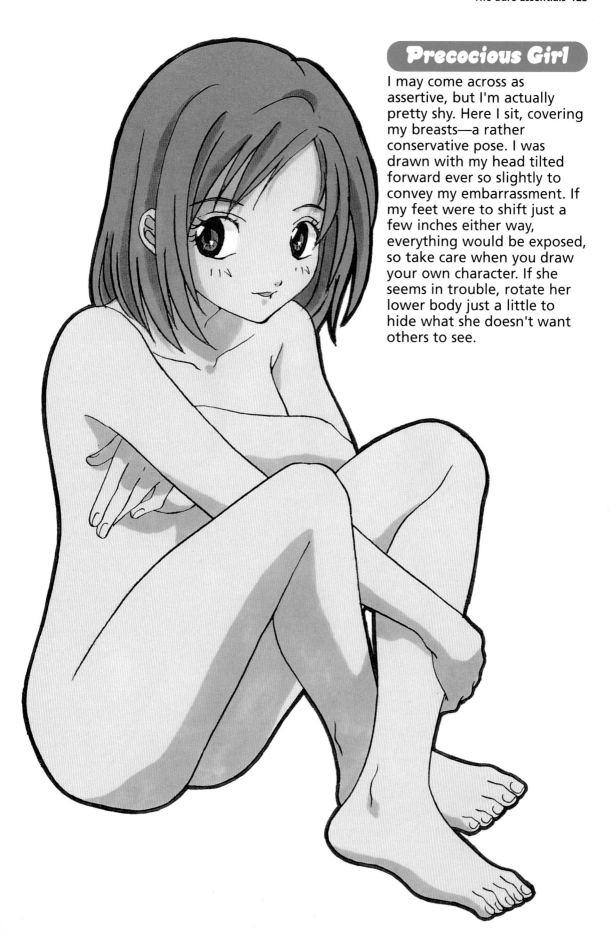

Uppity Girl

This is a painful pose to hold. I have confidence in my figure, and I can be quite aggressive. I am looking askance, which is supposed to make me seem coquettish. If you are striving to create a seductive atmosphere, a pose such as this is just perfect.

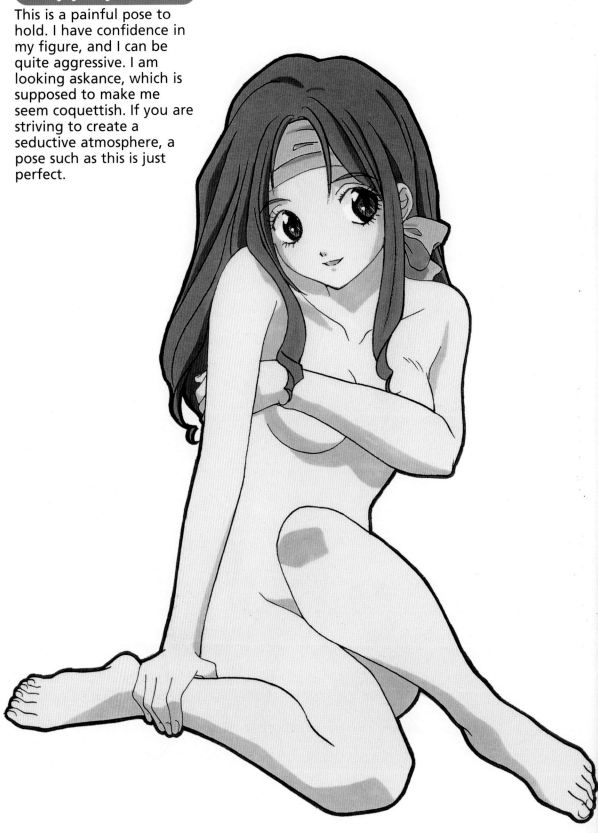

No Boys Allowed!

Chapter 5

The Girls Restroom

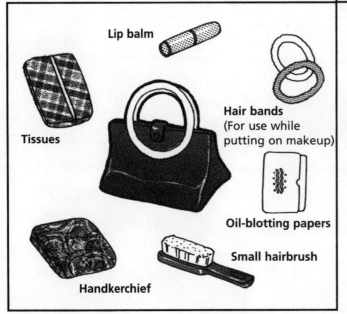

Lip balm

Tissues

Hair bands
(For use while
putting on makeup)

Oil-blotting papers

Small hairbrush

Handkerchief

The tiny shelves above the sinks in a girls restroom are usually covered with a wide assortment of personal effects. The most common is the makeup case, whose contents consist of various items for touching up a girl's appearance. Other items that can be found on these shelves include tissues (after girls apply lipstick, they put a piece of tissue between their lips and press down to blot excess lipstick and produce a matte finish), brushes, and hairclips to hold back bangs while applying makeup. The reason girls take so long in the restroom is because they are so busy making themselves look great!

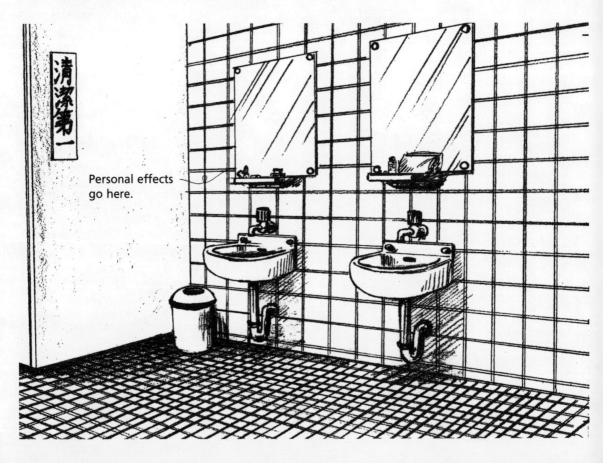

Personal effects go here.

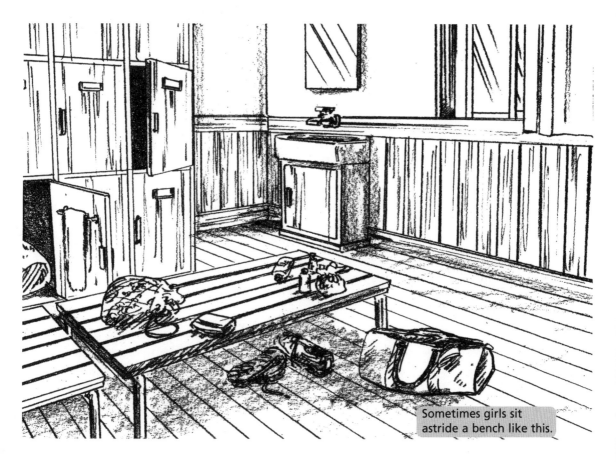

Sometimes girls sit astride a bench like this.

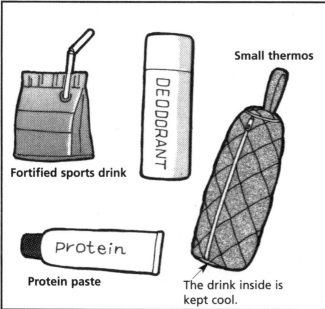

Fortified sports drink

Small thermos

DEODORANT

Protein paste

protein

The drink inside is kept cool.

This is a girls locker room. It's a dull room with wood furnishings, but with all of the personal effects scattered about, it takes on a colorful glow. Since this is strictly girls' world, its occupants tend to wash, powder and shave in the boldest ways imaginable. The bench is also strewn with articles: a fortified sports drink, a change of underwear, a deodorant spray for after sports practice (and a shower). Their conversations are bolder here than when in the outside world. They show each other their underwear, and they compare figures.

The Girls Locker Room

Lingerie Shops

Of course, no one has actually banished young men from lingerie shops. However, any male seen wandering about in the store will definitely receive a few dubious glances. Some stores place bargain tables near their entrance, causing women to flock enthusiastically to them. Such boutiques usually sell both domestic and import brands, and often the designs are luxurious and seductive. Inside the store, scrumptious fragrances from potpourri sprays and sachets waft through the air. Stunning store clerks seem to be de rigueur. Their shapely figures act as advertising for form-sculpting, support undergarments (pushup bras and girdles). These seem to be what the girls wear when looking to brace up their "secret weapons."

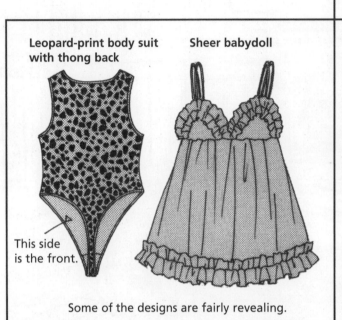

Leopard-print body suit with thong back

Sheer babydoll

This side is the front.

Some of the designs are fairly revealing.

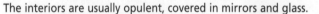

The interiors are usually opulent, covered in mirrors and glass.

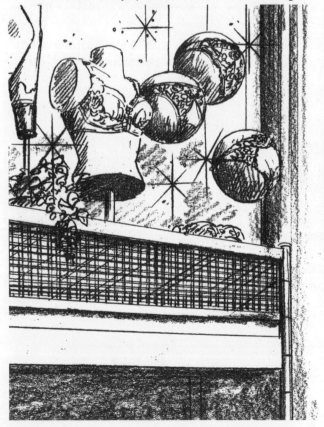
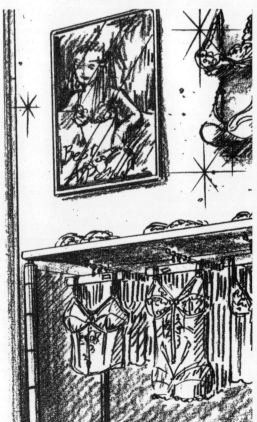

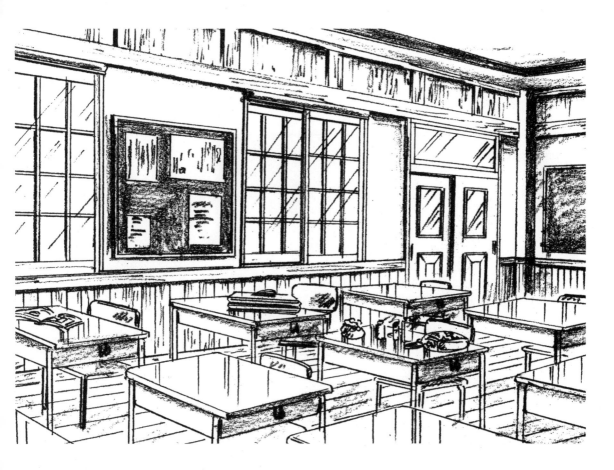

The girls-only classroom is definitely a place where a boy does not set foot. Out of the sight of boys, even the most seemingly mousy girl transforms into a ferocious chatterbox. The classroom hits a boisterous peak at lunchtime. Since these are still growing girls, they have surprisingly voracious appetites. The more energetic girls often buy a muffin and some milk at the school store. Some girls secretly snack before lunchtime, and then purchase a few rice balls when the lunch bell rings. Many of the girls bring lunches their mothers made, but there are always a few girls who made their own. Most girls bring their lunches in plastic boxes held in a kinchaku (drawstring sack) or wrapped in an oversized handkerchief. They also typically use forks and spoons (there are so many cute ones sold in the stores) rather than chopsticks. Some girls share homemade cakes and cookies.

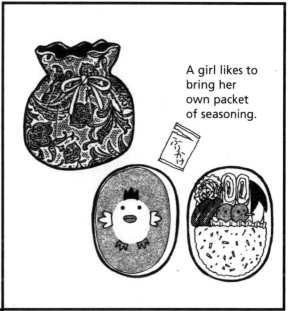

A girl likes to bring her own packet of seasoning.

Lunchtime

Spas

Even when girls go on a group vacation, they spend forever in the bath. "What exactly are they doing in there?" the boys wonder. Ladies' hot-spring baths are constructed no differently from the men's. Once the girls warm up, they take their time shampooing, soaping up, washing off, and then repeating the process all over again. They compare breasts and exchange exercise tips. When feeling flushed, they shower and cool off while sitting on the edge of the communal bath. Since most of the complimentary shampoo and soap products provided by the hotel are of low quality, girls usually bring their own. Surprisingly enough, even the girls shyest about taking off their clothes will prance about in the changing room, boldly drying themselves off from their baths.

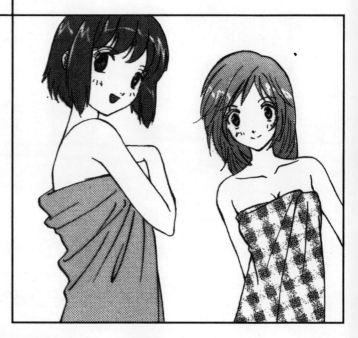

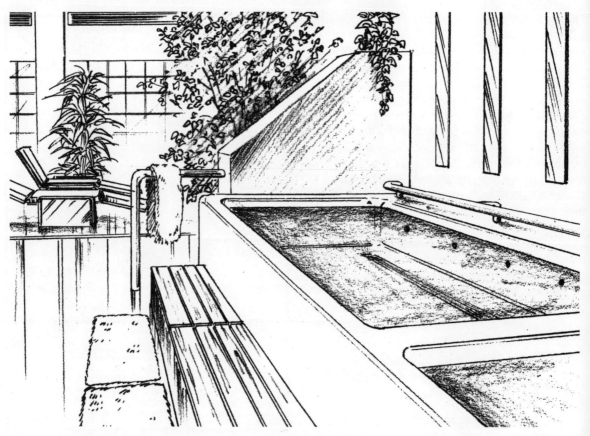

Afterword

I began this project, which consisted of more than 100 pages, all illustrated, and some in color, doubting that I could actually meet the deadline. I finished just over a month later than promised, and I didn't get much sleep during those final days. Naturally, I had to give up video games. (Ouch!) I thought I would collapse from exhaustion. It was during this time that a number of my friends, including my husband, joined the battle in various forms. I would like to express my eternal gratitude to each and every one.

Superficially, this volume is a collection of sample drawings. However, the book's function changes depending on the eye of the beholder. I would like to stress that the drawings at best represent my (humble) style, and that I hope the reader is able to take from this book the method of representation and expression best suited to him or her and does not blindly swallow hook, line and sinker everything herein.

Finally, I would like to express my appreciation to the editors, Ms. Hyakutake and Mr. Shirokura, as well as the rest of the staff, for their extreme patience and calm in putting up with me and my bizarre needs. Thank you.

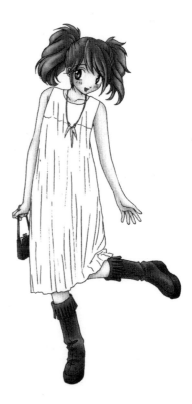